COALSEAM

COALSEAM

Poems from the Anthracite Region

SECOND EDITION

Edited by
Karen Blomain

With a Foreword by
Frank MacShane

SCRANTON: UNIVERSITY OF SCRANTON PRESS

© 1996 by University of Scranton Press

University of Scranton Press
Editorial Office:
Linden & Monroe
Scranton, PA 18510

Coalseam : poems from the anthracite region / edited by Karen
Blomain; with a foreword by Frank MacShane. – 2nd ed.
   p. cm.
ISBN 0-940866-54-4
   1. American poetry–Pennsylvania–Schuylkill River Valley.
2. Coal mines and mining–Pennsylvania–Schuylkill River Valley-
-Poetry. 3. Anthracite coal–Pennsylvania–Schuylkill River Valley-
-Poetry. 4. Schuylkill River Valley (Pa.)–Poetry. 5. American
poetry–20th century. I. Blomain, Karen, 1944- .
PS548.P4C63 1996
811' .54080327981–dc20   95-53758
                                      CIP

Marketing and Distribution
Fordham University Press
University Box L
Bronx, NY 10458

PRINTED IN THE UNITED STATES OF AMERICA

To the memory of my grandparents: Ernest and Anna Hein Watkins and Emile and Maude Kielty Blomain, whose evocative tales and lovingly preserved sense of history were responsible for this book . . .

. . . and to my friend, Ernst Koch.

A very special note of gratitude to Craig Czury who was there the entire time with good ideas, frequent help, much deserved prodding, and constant encouragement . . .

. . . and to the Djerassi Foundation, the Ragdale Foundation, and Blue Mountain Center where I was given the time and space first to dream this project, then to complete it.

CONTENTS

Foreword   xiii

Introduction   1

Part I: "I come from coal"

Anthracite History   13
CRAIG CZURY

I Come from Coal   14
MAGGIE CHELLAND MARTIN

Burning Mountain   15
W. S. MERWIN

"All, they said, would venture it together"   16
PAUL KELLEY

"The Hollow City"   18
PAUL KELLEY

Slag Valley   19
THOMAS KIELTY BLOMAIN

My Mother at Evening   19
HARRY HUMES

Centralia   21
KAREN BLOMAIN

Coal Train   23
JAY PARINI

Part II: "Two blasts and the windows shake"

Working the Face   27
JAY PARINI

Old Man Müller   28
NANCY DEISROTH

A Rosary for Dad in the Asylum   32
EDWARD MORAN

Shamokin   36
CRAIG CZURY

The Blind Man 36
BIM ANGST

The River 38
PAUL KELLEY

Playing in the Mines 40
JAY PARINI

Giving It Up for Lent 40
EDWARD MORAN

The Dancers 41
KAREN BLOMAIN

Delaware Lackawanna Diesel Running Through 43
HELEN RUGGIERI

At the Counting House of Buck Run Mine 44
HARRY HUMES

Dog Hole 45
THOMAS KIELTY BLOMAIN

Walking the Trestle 47
JAY PARINI

Rotten Angel 47
GERALD STERN

For a Russian Mother 49
BIM ANGST

Tanya 50
JAY PARINI

Making Soap 52
NANCY DEISROTH

Walking the Anthracite 53
HARRY HUMES

Genetti Hotel 54
CRAIG CZURY

Elvis, My Life, and the Real Madonna 55
MAGGIE CHELLAND MARTIN

Part III: "Bells like sad angels"

Lackawanna 61
W. S. MERWIN

TABLE OF CONTENTS ix

Father and Mother 62
ANTHONY PETROSKY

Among School Children 74
CRAIG CZURY

Learning to Read 75
HELEN RUGGIERI

Fire 77
MAGGIE CHELLAND MARTIN

Pedlar 79
NANCY DEISROTH

Buying Pagan Babies 79
KAREN BLOMAIN

Bottled-Up 80
MAGGIE CHELLAND MARTIN

Nanticoke Bus 84
CRAIG CZURY

Hospital View 85
KAREN BLOMAIN

The Red Coal 86
GERALD STERN

Morning, Years after the Mining 88
THOMAS KIELTY BLOMAIN

Bells Like Sad Angels 89
CRAIG CZURY

The Miner's Wife Leaves Home 90
KAREN BLOMAIN

A Christmas Poem 92
HELEN RUGGIERI

The Photograph 93
HARRY HUMES

In Andy Gavin's on St. Patrick's Day 94
THOMAS KIELTY BLOMAIN

Hacking and Smoking 95
CRAIG CZURY

Easter 96
BIM ANGST

Going for Water   97
    NANCY DEISROTH
Confession   98
    BIM ANGST

Part IV: "From the face of the vein"

The Harvest   103
    KAREN BLOMAIN
Huckleberry Woman   104
    W. S. MERWIN
The Bootleg Coal Hole   105
    HARRY HUMES
Mango   106
    KAREN BLOMAIN
Robbing the Pillars   107
    HARRY HUMES
Bones & Ashes   108
    HELEN RUGGIERI
Photo Finish   109
    EDWARD MORAN
Coal Pickers   110
    HARRY HUMES
Baron Legacy   111
    THOMAS KIELTY BLOMAIN
Sickness   112
    BIM ANGST
The Wheels of the Trains   113
    W. S. MERWIN
Carbondale Cave-In   114
    KAREN BLOMAIN
The Miner's Wake   115
    JAY PARINI
Astronomy Lesson in Ashley, Pennsylvania   116
    EDWARD MORAN
Thinking about Shelley   117
    GERALD STERN

TABLE OF CONTENTS

Kulpmont Hearsay Tales   118
    CRAIG CZURY
So the Coal Was Gone   122
    THOMAS KIELTY BLOMAIN

List of Contributors   123

FOREWORD

It would be hard to imagine a landscape more ravaged than the countryside that runs through the Schuylkill Valley of Pennsylvania. The very names that mark the settlements of Port Carbon, Minersville and Coaldale reflect the grim lives of the men and women who over the years have worked the anthracite mines and managed to raise families in a hostile and remorseless setting.

Mining has long been associated with exploitation and ugliness. It tends to harden the soul as well as the spirit of those who work underground and have few prospects of improving their lives. Whether they work in the gold mines of South Africa, the salt mines of Egypt, or the coal mines of Germany and America, they are subject to people who control them. Physically they are among the strongest people in the world, but since they are generally uneducated, they often have been forced to accept minimal wages.

Today, stories of the Molly McGuires, who fought for better conditions for miners at the turn of the century, are still part of the heritage of the Schuylkill Valley, as are memories of the terrible influenza epidemic of 1918 which took the lives of thousands of people in the region.

The novelist John O'Hara was only a boy at this time, visiting the small towns of Pennsylvania with his father who, as a doctor, was trying to help those he could. One of the houses young O'Hara visited was cluttered with "rubber boots, tin cans and the framework of an abandoned baby carriage," while the kitchen reeked of "the awful stink of cabbage and dirty feet." There were four young children in one bed and the doctor soon realized that they were infected with diphtheria. In time, the mother understood that one had died so she began to rock back and forth, "kissing her and looking up at us with fat streams of tears running from her eyes. She would stop crying for a second, but would start again, crying with her mouth open and the tears, unheeded, sliding in over her upper lip."

The worst part of living in such a place and time was that so little could be done to help. But there were also moments of joy and promise that kept the miners and their families from despair. Their commitment to their neighbors and friends, and to the place where they lived, gave them the courage to keep on living. Coming to this harsh world of mining pits from Lithuania, Ireland, Poland, Portugal, and Germany, they were forgotten by the world beyond the mines, but they turned to one another for the courage and the strength that allowed them to survive.

As the poems in this collection show, the people of this region and their successors overcame their difficulties and regained their composure as they told their own stories and recorded their lives and the worth of all who lived in this valley. Their heritage is as fine as anyone's in the country and their history as valuable, for they reflect the strength of the human spirit and their own determination.

FRANK MacSHANE

INTRODUCTION

I was not to read Dante for twelve years, but at the age of six I had a perfect image of the landscape of the *Inferno* and knew the hopelessness and terror of its inhabitants, those grim faces cast in red shadows of flame and obscured by smoke. I saw it the first time in a mine cave and recognized that same terror in the tales of my neighbors and the episodes in the family history book throughout my childhood in Archbald, a small town in the anthracite region of Pennsylvania. By 1952 when I was eight years old, mining had all but ceased, but the scars remained both on the land and the people.

The images of that landscape permeated my consciousness and provided the metaphors and a language I would use in my writing. The poet William Pitt Root observed, "The landscape you grow up in—be it in the Bronx, the Everglades or the Sahara—constitutes a kind of primordial reality for each person. You will never find a place more real than the one you grew up in, where your eyes are new and just opening."

Over the past five years I have met other poets who write from the same locus. Studying their work, I have come to see a rich diversity in the development of the idea of place, of that particular place. In 1988 I visited Centralia, the famous "town on fire." I went with the hope of rediscovering my connection to the reality and metaphor of my childhood. Preparing this anthology was another path to that affirmation.

*   *   *

The anthracite region of northeastern Pennsylvania extends into seven counties, 484 square miles underlaid with rich veins of hard coal—anthracite, as it is more commonly known. Seventy-five percent of the world's anthracite was found in this small area. The coal lies in three long, boat-shaped beds between mountains spanning an area from Forest City to Schickshinny (North Seam), White Haven to Macadoo (East Seam), and Shenandoah to Williamstown (South Seam).

For 160 years coal had been deep-mined in the same way—tunnels dug into the vein, the coal scored to hold explosive charges, a blast to break up the solid mass of coal, then the removal of the loose coal to the surface. Both above and below ground the landscape of mining is terrifying—long corridors of glistening black rocks, scurrying rats, the smell of smoke and sulfur, clotted air, intolerable heat, mules born and bred in the mines who never saw daylight, canaries used to detect deadly gas buildup and, always, the fear of taking too much from an unforgiving nature—the resulting cave-in. The miner's lot was so terrible that during medieval times it was considered an occupation fit only for slaves. All the toiling and danger during these twelve-hour days was done in a world which had abolished light because of the impenetrable dust which the miners inhaled constantly.

A view of the inside of the mine, the actual work of mining, is given in glimpses throughout this anthology. But poets are not the only writers who described the almost surreal picture of the miners' daily reality. Stephen Crane explains what he saw inside a mine: "After a time we came upon two men crouching where the roof of the passage came near to meeting the floor. If the picture could have been brought to where it would have the opposition and the contrast of the glorious summer-time earth, it would have been a grim and ghastly thing. The garments of the men were not more sable than their faces, and when they turned their heads to regard our tromping party, their eyeballs and teeth shone white as bleached bones. It was like the grinning of two skulls there in the shadows. The tiny lamps in their hats made a trembling light that left weirdly shrouded the movement of their limbs and bodies. We might have been confronting terrible specters." The horrible conditions in the mines, the abuses by greedy owners and bosses led to widespread discontent and eventually the development of organized resistance groups like the Molly Maguires. The Mollies waged a war of terror against the mine owners which culminated in 1877 with the hanging of a famous gang in Pottsville and Mauch Chunk for the murder of the mine boss John P. Jones. "Powderkeg" Kerrigan, who escaped hanging when he turned state's evidence against his co-conspirators, wrote this crude verse:

> I think I will lay down my pen when I say a word to ye,
> That's to quit drinking liquor and keeping company,
> For if you don't you will rue it until the day you die,
> So Kerrigan, now, with a glad heart, says to you all
> Good-bye.

Ironically, during the period that the Mollies were awaiting execution, mining disasters continued to plague the area. In *The Pennsylvania Sampler*, Paul S. Beers notes that there was an "explosion at the nearby Wadesville shaft. Eight children were left fatherless, and some of the remains of newlywed Thomas Connors of Summit Hill were taken home to his bride in his dinner can."

Mining in the United States had its heyday from 1890 to 1950. During that time the expanding industry was fueled by a steady stream of immigrant workers. Social historian Peter Roberts examined the demographics of the area: "In 1900 it (the percentage of foreign born residents) had reached 46.36%. Boys as young as six were routinely put to work in the mines."

Life in the small towns that grew up around the mouth of the mines was bleak. The immigrant population lived like slaves in company-owned houses. Often the company had paid the workers' passage to America, advanced them money to settle, rented them houses, and gave them credit at the company-owned "pluck me" store. Sadly, the immigrants who had come with optimism and hope for a new life often found themselves hopelessly indebted and trapped, literally slaves to the large debts they had contracted and could not repay.

The work of mining was inherently and notoriously dangerous. Beers notes, "In 1894, Pennsylvania's 140,000 hard-coal miners produced 51 million tons of coal, and 446 men were killed. . . . In 1907, there were 708 hard coal miners killed. From 1870 to 1968 Pennsylvania had 31,047 known fatalities in the anthracite mines."

Poet Harry Humes, who grew up in a mining family in Girardville, observes, "Sirens were always going off. Mine accidents were common. My grandfather lost an arm and wore a primitive artificial device, the result of which was that the men in my family have ever since been called Hook. A friend's father who'd take us fishing had coal dust embedded permanently in his face as the result of a dynamite explosion."

In 1900, Mother Jones, who had spent months in the anthracite fields organizing the United Mine Workers, was not speaking hyperbolically when she often referred to the anthracite miners as "the slaves of the caves." The miners and their families had little hope to change their lot, and even less to gain the understanding of those who had come before them and had power over their lives.

The mining towns themselves were geographically isolated from each other by mountains. An aerial view shows villages strung like beads in gullies between ridges. As a result, there was little communication between neighboring towns. Within the communities themselves, sections were rigidly delineated by nationality. The Irish, Welsh, Slovak, Polish, Czech, and later Italian miners lived in separate sections of town. As is often the case when people are faced with impossible conditions, lack of security, tumultuous change and ever-present danger, the miners and their families held passionately to the only security they knew—their native culture, language and religion. In that sense, the miners' settlements were similar to the city ghetto cultures that formed at the same time. Fearful and skeptical of each other, these cultures lived side by side without mingling.

Most of the miners were Roman Catholic. Here, as in Europe, religion was one stable reality. But even within the same church, separate cultures were strictly maintained. Some towns had more than one church, each with its own ethnic identity. The smaller one-church towns frequently had an Irish, a Polish and an Italian priest. Each said Mass and heard confessions in his own language and conducted services in the tradition of his country. The religious cultures—their festivals and patron saints, foods, customs, even the dates of holidays—were scrupulously maintained as they were in the old country.

The lives and customs of the miners and their families were greatly misunderstood even by those few who sought to study them. In his book *Anthracite Coal Communities*, Peter Rogers, Ph.D., reports "The Sclav [sic] is proverbial for his indifference to sickness and death" and that "Such callousness is simply barbarous and connotes a low stage of civilization." In his discussion of mine-workers from both Anglo-Saxon and Sclav stock he explains "The Sclav is a good machine in the hands of competent directors. . . . He thinks slowly and is willing to follow the lead of others."

Part of the transplanted culture which thrived in the anthracite area was the strong, lyrical, oral traditional forms—work chants, ballads, and religious verse which captured the immigrant experiences. In the same way that landscape connects with and enriches art, the poet is further favored if the landscape has its own language, an idiom and diction of its obsessions and technologies. As a result, mining becomes not simply the subject matter but often the driving metaphor behind many of the poems. Indeed, at times mining becomes a metaphor for writing. Words and phrases like *culm, patch, slag, breaker, colliery, black damp, robbing, weightman, tag and hook, vein, slate, pea, dog hole,* and *shaft* are a strong part of the consciousness of place.

Yet all of the writers in this anthology would caution that overdependence on this vocabulary can easily devalue it. One of the strengths of the poems collected here is that the specific language of place is used sparingly and naturally. The poems illustrate the diversity, complexity, and virtuosity of poets from the anthracite region. Their use of subject matter, language, and form is as disparate as their personal obsessions. The forms of these poems range from ballads to work chants, from documentary to lyric, from abstract to concrete. What the poets have in common is a fascination with the hole in the ground, the mine, the images and language it provides, the lives and cultures that surround it as well as what the process of mining means both literally and metaphorically. Jay Parini is fond of quoting G. K. Chesterton's remark that every writer has an ideal landscape at the back of his imagination. Parini considers the anthracite region that ideal landscape—"a trove of bright and dark scenes, similes, tropes of initiation and development, of loss and inexplicable joy."

By 1950, deep mining for anthracite was dwindling rapidly. Since then, the only active mining has taken place in illegal coal holes, small operations, and stripping pits where the landscape is chewed to pieces by huge machines operated by a few men from the relative safety of a control cab. The scars remain; the dream persists. The landscape is alive in the groves of white birch, contrasting with the slag heaps from which they sprout, and in the works of these poets who honor the past and the present of the anthracite region.

Anthony Petrosky mused recently, "Although I haven't

been in a mine since I was a kid, the issues affecting the lives of miners still don't seem to me to have changed. It was always the bosses trying to get as much as they could from the miners who had so little. Never understood it. A couple of years ago my father gave me Jurgis's (his grandfather's) five-foot steel pick that he used everyday. It weighs about 15–20 pounds, and as hard as it is to imagine his digging that into the coalseams everyday all his life, he did, and my writing about him and our family was my way of letting it be known that our family lived that way for a time, and it was a hard life that pulled people together and pushed them apart with a ferocity that I have not seen anywhere else." Petrosky's statement echoes those by other contributors who celebrate, condemn, and ultimately comprehend as they write.

Blessedly, of that life comes art and the validation and solace it provides. Edward Moran speaks of the recognition of native images: "I did not encounter Franz Kline, for example, until adulthood, in a Saturday afternoon epiphany at New York's Museum of Modern Art. The catalog referred to his debt to Japanese calligraphy, but I knew better. He was from Wilkes-Barre, sure as black lung. His ebony slashes were not sumi brush strokes: they were the charred timbers of the mine workings on Stanton Street, the underground support pillars of Glen Alden, the Huber Colliery in Ashley, the blasted-out pits of Avondale. Homeboys know the dark satanic mills that weaned us."

It is not just the hard mining life that these pages honor. They are, in large measure, given over to the ordinariness of life, the beautiful common moments which, although they might have happened anywhere, happened there, at that particular moment, to that particular person. The person happened to be a poet who, following the dictum of William Stafford, believes it is a writer's province not so much to invent as to notice. The ordinary, beautiful moment brings with it the scent of specific memories, "The smell of citronella on quiet summer nights that faded away a long time ago, and the taste of strawberry ice cream from Woodlawn Dairy. Most of all, I remember the mantle of sulfur haze that clotted the air on damp rainy days and hot nights in summer. The burning culm that lit the sky, a strange looming volcano never meant to erupt—only burn—slowly, steadily. It directed our lives," recalls Maggie Chelland Martin.

In the act of compiling this anthology, I realized once again the value of writing from place, both the shared voice and the small idiosyncratic glimpses which this group of poets has provided. In *A River Runs Through It* Norman MacLean says, "I am haunted by water. I am haunted by that small mining town. It is the place that helps me feel more at home in this unsettling world, and bedrock to all my writing." I hope that in these pages the reader smells that damp, sweet evening, hears sad angels and enters the place where these writers' eyes first opened.

COALSEAM

I

"I come from coal"

ANTHRACITE HISTORY

Craig Czury

U p this steep hill the old rowhouses:
tar shingle,
kitchen still on the ground floor.

And the cemetery overlooking a stripping pit:

Nelabovage * Zlotsky * Osepovich
* Matuliawiczius * Paczkoskie

In the History Book of this region
only the clearly pronounced German names
and the Anglos with their round pictures:
President of the Bank, Owner of the Coal Company,
the merchants . . .

The very clean wives of the social club.

And in the photo of miners at the colliery
they write: "Coaldirt"

Wojtkiewicz * Bzura * Pszeniczny
* Marcincavage * Zlotorzynskas * Andro
Csuri * Masijauskas * Pultynovich . . .

Coaldirt.

I COME FROM COAL

Maggie Chelland Martin

My ears resound with the sound of coal
avalanching down the metal chute
into the basement coal bin
gleaming blue-black
common gems
falling over one another
loudly piling up and up
as I stood watching
fearing I'd be swallowed by them
never to breathe again
my mouth packed tight
with rounded chunks of darkness

Saved by the shriek of metal
as the chute withdrew
I sucked in a breath
and plunged into the mound with my shovel
taming the pile
while my father fed the furnace
its mouth gaping
fiery tongues lashing
red hot nuggets crackling
like the fires of hell

I come from coal
My bones are filled with marrow black
liquid carbon fills my veins
the legacy of men whose faces never saw the light of day
whose lungs were filled with pockets filled with dust

whose hearts beat out a rhythm
as they dug into the earth's jet core

My mouth tastes of the waiting
the ritual of women who listened for the warning sound
the shattering of the shaft
as they birthed the children, cooked the meals
pretending not to wait.

BURNING MOUNTAIN

W. S. Merwin

No blacker than others in winter, but
The hushed snow never arrives on that slope.
An emanation of steam on damp days,
With a faint hiss, if you listen some places,
Yes, and if you pause to notice, an odor,
Even so near the chimneyed city, these
Betray what the mountain has at heart. And all night,
Here and there, popping in and out of their holes
Like groundhogs gone nocturnal, the shy flames.

Unnatural, but no mystery.
Many are still alive to testify
Of the miner who left his lamp hanging
Lit in the shaft and took the lift, and never
Missed a thing till, halfway home to supper
The bells' clangor caught him. He was the last
You'd have expected such a thing from;
The worrying kind, whose old-womanish
Precautions had been a joke for years.
Smothered and silent, for some miles the fire

Still riddles the fissured hill, deviously
Wasting and inextinguishable. They
Have sealed off all the veins they could find.
Thus at least setting limits to it, we trust.
It consumes itself; but so slowly it will outlast
Our time and our grandchildren's, curious
But not unique: there was always one of these
Nearby, wherever we moved, when I was a child.

Under it, not far, the molten core
Of the earth recedes from its thin crust
Which all the fires we light cannot prevent
From cooling. Not a good day's walk above it
The meteors burn out in the air to fall
Harmless in empty fields, if at all.
Before long it practically seemed normal.
With its farms on it, and wells of good water,
Still cold, that should last us, and our grandchildren.

"ALL, THEY SAID, WOULD VENTURE IT
❧ TOGETHER"

—Walam Olum

Paul Kelley

My father's voice
          was asking, was wanting
          to know
               there *was* before, they
were not the only ones,
they were not
always here, these people, this land
did not always hold them up, they came
westward as part of a movement of people from

eastern coastal cities inland for land
from Connecticut New York New Jersey
into "The Beautiful Valley" in ones & twos
& by the score: Smith, Abbots—Phillip & James—
Reuben Taylor, Isaac Trip, Howe, Slocums,
Fellows, Joseph, Enoch Holmes, Daniel Wademan,
Duwain, Von Storch, Obediah Gore,
Drinker, Henry, Wurtses, and later,
Scrantons, and later still
hundreds and thousands more
not mentioned nor remembered
as the quanta rolled up
It was land
they were after, at first, when
the land was oak, & and pine trees so thick
they called the place Dark Hollow,
air to breathe, clear water, abundance,
space they could spread out
in, & put wheat into the land, to make
a new beginning or was it
soon after, by 1828,
it was all different it was coal
that brought them here, coal
the land was sought for, abundance
no longer of the labor the fruit the land yielded
profit now in dollars coal
to fuel the fires of iron & steel &
railroads Industry with a big I
Lackawanna Station standing in a wheat field
steel tracks
& all newness gone to King Coal
        & the people to mine it
& to lay the track, to forge, to work
to make industry, machines, imported

as materials, their many languages
used by their employers to keep them
apart, these people from Wales,
Ireland, Poland, England,
Germany, Russia, & Italy
the "olde world"
  come together here
which americans
   & the Lenni Lenape, who
   were renamed "Delaware" after an English
   baron, were forced, went quietly,
   west, & disappeared there, Wissler says
     the land
     & the people
     & the coal
     & the city
a voice asking
was wanting to know.

"THE HOLLOW CITY"

Paul Kelley ✵

It shall be known as "The Hollow City,"
as until the 1960s when the flushing
of the tunnels with culm began & closed off
 large sections, a man could go into the earth
in Southside, & walk from there, through
the earth, all the way beneath it, & come out
in Dickson City. Without ever coming to the surface,
he could walk Southside, Central City, Pine Brook,
Green Ridge, Providence, & on: the distance
of the city. And he could hear there,

along the way, the ringing of the bells
of trolleys running on Pittston Avenue,
or the bells of classes changing
in the schools, or, if it were a Sunday
morning, the voices of people singing
in the churches above him.

SLAG VALLEY

Thomas Kielty Blomain

I've seen the old men from the slag valley
wearing their worn gray caps
inhaling Lucky Strike and anthracite
congregating at the aluminum-sided bars
that line the dim street with familiar signs.
I've seen them malinger
outside vast cathedral doors
fidgety as children
in parochial Easter suits,
their catechism
on earth's dusty shelf
a bound history
of culm mountains.

MY MOTHER AT EVENING

Harry Humes

This evening with the breeze
blowing the curtains from the window,
my mother tells me again

19

the story of her young husband,
when they first lived in the Ash Alley house,
no children, no car, her hair red,
and him with his first good mining
at Packer Number five, then miles from home,
how at the end of his shift
he'd come up from the pit in the gunboat,
face black, lips and tongue pink as her peonies,
and not stopping at the washroom,
walk down to the railroad tracks
and wait for a train to hop.

Lunch bucket and tin water bottle
rattling on ropes around his neck,
he'd run alongside when one came through
and reaching up over the steel wheels
for the ladder, haul himself up
the side of the car, and hang there
for the ride back, hoping the train
would not gather too much speed
on the Ashland grade.
Sometimes it did, she tells me again,
and then he'd go right on through.

Not married a year,
her eyes then clear; hair shining,
and a blue bandanna rolled
and tied around her head.
She would sit by the tracks
humming one of the old hymns,
her hand on the cold rail,
and watching for the signal
at the grade crossing,
for the engine's powerful lamp
to make everything blaze as it passed,

for him to swing down, smiling,
out of the dark.

I think of them then,
walking down along the path,
down into the evening,
a few bats over town,
some children playing hoop-the-lalla
beneath a street light,
and my mother and her young husband
passing by, almost touching.

 CENTRALIA

(October 31, 1986)

Karen Blomain

Underground the fire, wild
and consuming breathes through sinkholes

punctured in the earth's cheek. Near town
the makeshift billboard, "Centralia mine

fire—Our future" the road seeps, tar
glitters from the unremitting heat.

Half the town already sold and moved,
the holdouts turn around three times

prepare for the long draft of winter.
After All Hollow's Eve yards crust, furrows

fallow until spring, and sparks along the berm
leap, subside and leap again like ideas

21

we forget, recall in turn,
within the locus of mild superstitions.

Nearby the graveyard awaits the offices
of flames which darted once to twenty feet.

Nature's taste for irony. Caught
in the gauze of headlights, the uneven

stones warn with the same eloquence as empty
houses. Half of one street dark already,

the neighbors gone, windows covered with
sheets of paneling, porches uncluttered.

The new wood a seasonal riot: pumpkins,
goblins, a witch and two leggy skeletons,

defacings layer upon layer. Next door,
a hoop, a fleet of bikes in the yard,

and the fluorescent blur and mutter
of a screen, in an upstairs window

a woman concentrates at a sewing machine.
Under the streetlight, teens in concert

shirts hurl grenades of toilet paper,
festoon the interlock of wires.

Imagine the corner bar, some shouting,
cheering, maybe for a game, where

anything might come of anger. Imagine
the quiet neighbor cutting wood

to seal his front door after him, measuring
the exact distance from his parents'

old transplanted dream. Imagine neatness
as consolation, each corner true

enough that he might come back years from now,
retrieve the childhood hidden in these walls.

Listen to his stumbling Polish, a prayer
for meals, the only one he can recall.

Imagine his wife, checking the truck
packed and idling at the curb, walking

back into her garden. Imagine
a pie tin scarecrow, stubble

of pruned roses, the rot of cabbage,
a withered arbor, the eyes of sunflowers.

COAL TRAIN

Jay Parini

Three times a night it woke you
in middle summer, the Erie Lackawanna,
running to the north on thin, loud rails.
You could feel it coming a long way off:
at first, a tremble in your belly,
a wire trilling in your veins, then diesel
rising to a froth beneath your skin.
You could see the cowcatcher,
wide as a mouth and eating ties,
the headlight blowing a dust of flies.
There was no way to stop it.
You lay there, fastened to the tracks

and waiting, breathing like a bull,
your fingers lit at the tips like matches.
You waited for the thunder of wheel and bone,
the axles sparking, fire in your spine.
Each passing was a kind of death,
the whistle dwindling to a ghost in air,
the engine losing itself in trees.
In a while, your heart was the loudest thing,
your bed was a pool of night.

II

"Two blasts, and the windows shake"

WORKING THE FACE

Jay Parini

O n his belly with a coal pick
mining underground:
the pay was better for one man
working the face.
Only one at a time could get
so close, his nose
to the anthracite, funneling
light from a helmet, chipping,
with his eyes like points of fire.
He worked, a taproot
tunneling inward, layer
by layer, digging
in a world of shadows,
thick as a slug against the floor,
dark all day long.
Wherever he turned, the facets
showered a million stars.
He was prince of darkness,
stalking the village at 6 P.M.,
having been to the end of it,
core and pith
of the world's rock belly.

OLD MAN MÜLLER

Nancy Deisroth ❧

I can't sleep, Doc,
My heart pounds so.
Can't you hear it?
I'm afraid to close my eyes.

Name? Muller, George.
In the old country it was
Müller. Georg Müller.
Here it's different—"easier,"
they say, "more American"; and I
wanted to be American.

How long I been like this?
Afraid to sleep?
Not since I was a kid
working in the mine.

Miner, yes. All my life.
I started as a door-boy
when I was twelve years old.
Sat there in the dark—
hours and hours—
alone except for rats that
sniffed around for my lunch.
I had a lamp, yes, but
oil was dear and I earned
only pennies that I gave over
to my mother.
I was the oldest boy.
There were eight of us:
six boys, two girls.

Three others died as babies.
My father, God rest his soul,
died when I was ten.
He was caught in a cave-in.
They brought him home in a
wheelbarrow; in a coma. They
wheeled him up to my mother and
dumped him on the ground.
"He's no more use to us," they said,
and left.
He died soon after and I
went to pick slate
up in the breaker.

I picked my fingers raw,
tossing bloody stones aside.
Their stones, *my* blood.
At night in my sleep I heard
the constant rumble of coal,
pouring down the chute between
my spread legs.
All night my back, my legs and feet
ached from the strain of sitting,
slumping, hours at a time,
braced against falling
into the sliding coal.
One day my buddy, Ed,
he got permission to pee.
He was gone a long time,
so they went after him.
They found him, all right,
caught up in the gears
that lifted the coal to fall
between our legs.

He must've slipped—it
was raining that day—
and fell in, and just kept
turning and turning
in the gear shaft.
No one heard him.
Hell, we stuck rags in our ears,
against the noise of the coal.
We got off early that day.
They had to shut down
to get his body out,
what was left of it.
They were pissed. They
lost half a day's work from us.

Well, so, then, when I was twelve,
I went downshaft with the men.
That cage ride was scary
when you dropped fast.
I'll never forget that sudden
falling away
as the hoist lowered us into the dark.
The first time, that sudden drop,
I dropped my lunch-pail; grabbed
the leg of an older man, a neighbor.
He put his arm around me, said
"It's all right, Georg."
I looked at that little cable . . . .

The men's head lamps shimmered,
you know, like candles at the
head of a casket. Like
at my father's casket.
I remember thinking that.
I'd take my lamp to the door

I had to tend, and I'd
hunker down into the damp.
I'd memorize the walls, the door,
and then blow out the light
to save on oil.
I told myself stories so
I wouldn't be afraid of the dark.

But I was afraid.
I had to listen for the mules
pulling the coal cars, and
get out of the way quick
when the door crashed open.
I knew kids got killed sometimes
when they fell asleep,
got smashed by a door.

See, the tunnels, it was clever,
they weren't just for getting
coal in and out, but for
ventilation, too, and those
doors—each one half the size
of a school bus—kept the air
going where it should. But
the air pressure. Sometimes I
struggled to close the door,
push it shut, against that pressure.
Hell, I was just a kid.
Anyway, most of the time
I'd just sit there, scared,
of the dark and the rats.
I was told more'n once,
"If the rats run out, follow 'em!"
But they were just always around,
stealing lunches when they could.

I usually went home by dinner-time, so
I carried only a water-bottle.

Sometimes I'd fall asleep listening
to the clank and ring of picks and
shovels, the grind of a drill, the
thumping boom of coal sliding, and
I'd wake up scared, my heart pounding
loud in my ears, like the coal.
I'd sit there sweating in the dark,
the damp, listening to my heart
and decide I must be still alive because
I could hear it.
Finally, far down the tunnel,
I'd see the flare of miner's lamps.
"Wake up, George," they'd holler.
"C'mon. Shift's over. Time for dinner."
We'd climb into the cage and I'd
watch that skinny cable hoist us up,
blinking, into the daylight.

Sorry, Doc, guess I tend to ramble on.
I'm just an old man, alone, and
I can't sleep. What do you think it is?
My heart pounds so; can't you hear it?
I'm afraid to close my eyes.

A ROSARY FOR DAD IN THE ASYLUM

Edward Moran ❖   Christmas, 1986

I have come to the place where they have laid you
    on a shelf
    smelling of orangepeel and tobacco

your mind knurled like beads
            your meds
            like threads
of ganglia that have come unraveled
like an unstrung rosary.

"Say a rosary for your father," called Mom from the porch
as I nosed from the curb.

Driving into Hazleton I strain at the car radio
like we used to in our nightkitchens
pulling in stations half the night
            WWVA in Wheeling
            WHAS in Louisville

then the "K's", crossing the Father of Waters
on the cold flat unseen but dreamed-of prairie nightback
—that west you showed me, Dad,
in your terror looking east
as on the night we pulled in Mexico
            sharing tongues dumb to us
            but how like Church Latin
XAR sputtering through the static ecstatic xtasy
and hot-blooded Mexico there in our coal-weary kitchen
and ashes at our feet for traction in the ice.

Turning the dial to please you
for your indulgence, Dad, not for time off in hell or
    purgatory
fingering the dial, stations like beads, threaded in air
I went for the scourging, the rising, the reigning
silent,
not incarnate,
but your beads were already rattling in your brain

unthreaded, no meds, frail threads
in a box of cries and voices.

The kitchen is the place for men in the night
in the cold, cold night when radio stations call from distant
towers
to kitchens
when the womenstuff of bread and garlic and roots
have been packed away

And you poured yourself into her,
   —my mother, your wife—
not grace but craze
and it dropped like a cross into my circled pool
and I finger dials, beads, knots of static
on my car radio, as your arrow trails comets into a sperm-
    rutted sky,
Now the decades have gone
and I search for you as the radio sputters glorias
from some coaltown gospel shop

I drive in avoidance,
round and round
seeking the source of the still firm signal
round and round the culm banks, the breaker rot
unwashed by the Father of Waters
trying not to get out of earshot, heirshot
of the circle of the arrow and the cross.

But when you drained yourself into her
   —my mother, your wife—
you touched my life
and our rosaries were cool potions
over my roots come alive
but the lessons of the blood you had not the tongue to tell

on the nightkitchen oilcloth, the chill
    and I hated you when you went mad
    —Hail, Full of Craze—
and me and my budding beads of spermroot swell
that drove me into cold pantries after the smell
    of the women had wisped to blaze.

Now the decades come full circle, the mysteries wild:
    announcement, loss and finding, the child
        stripped, defiled.

I find you at last, sag-grinned, still crazed
and your self drops like a cross into my hug
    (anchor now, not millstone)
so we float on clear radio pools awhirr
and when you drained yourself into her
    —my mother, your wife—
    you did it for dear life
        I know
        by now.

"I said a rosary for you," I dare,
thinking of Mom with the tangled clytemnestra in her
    hair,
        all sere.

Now the mysteries have been told,
the decades fold
around your brain that's knotted like a bead
the decades that, godspeed,
will wrap around your wrist
binding those hands that once flung bitter seed
    —no more a fist—
for I have come to the place where they have laid you
in ash and 'static amethyst'.

SHAMOKIN

Craig Czury

Even the pigeons have a deeper meaning,
cooing like the throaty gasp of a woman
under the tower of the old silkmill clock.

. . . the moon and the silkmill clock lit
by the same blood of the hour.

THE BLIND MAN

Bim Angst

Starry Joe had his hand blown off
mining fire 'cause he turned
to say "What?" when the fuse was too short.
'39's same to him as now and he don't
believe in rocket ships, but he knows dope
'cause the kids bagging school slip him joints
so he won't tell where they been. Joe's a
good mechanic. Blind, he feels them cranks
and gears with the stubs of that left hand
and holds things steady with the stump he likes
me to feel like some old prick it's all right
to show in public.

Joe's right eye ain't there at all
and he pops iron ball bearings, shinney chinkies, even
colored jawbreakers in there so I know he ain't shamed
of it. Deaf mostly, Starry Joe makes up words so
I don't hardly know what he's talking. Julie

runs round on him but he's got one son ain't hers
a lawyer somewhere I never heard who comes to pick
him up in a blue "ben-sadies-benz"
Sundays a couple times a summer.

His stump gets all blue in the cold
so blue you'd think it hurts, but he says no
it ain't hurt since he blew it off, but
he has me wrap it in a red t-shirt he uses to wipe oil
off his wrench, when he starts to feel his breath
freeze on his lip. He's scared it will fall
off and he won't be able to tell
'cause he can't feel it hurt.

His eye, the one that's left
is bigger'en any one I ever seen
bigger and black all the time like he's looking
always for things in the trees, up
like there's nothing under his feet, just up.

Sometimes he's real quiet and I don't
say a word. I'm careful even opening the door.
I sit and Joe paces, his stump
dragging the wall and back, the stump reaching
in air. He walks all day like that. I don't
say nothing, don't sneeze.

Sometimes it's so bad with him in there
I leave, sneaking quiet so he don't know
and then I just walk the store window
from outside, peeking in to watch and see he's o.k.

He stands in the middle of the floor, that stump out
that eye up, them legs just standing, him swaying
forward like his ankles was hammered to the floor

and I hear him through the window
humming soft to loud
like bees.

THE RIVER

Paul Kelley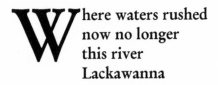

W here waters rushed
now no longer
this river
Lackawanna

Lechau-hanneck
      it enters the picture of this valley
      which takes its name from the river itself

at Uniondale and moves
southwesterly thru
         Forest City
       Simpson
          Carbondale
       Mayfield
      Jermyn
        Archbald
    Peckville
     Jessup
    Dickson City
    Scranton
  Moosic
Hughestown

drawing these towns together like knots
in its slow flow
it goes out, into

the Susquehanna at
                    Coxton, just north of
                    Pittston
& on, to Chesapeake Bay
        & the sea
the Shawnee & the Moosic
Mountains on either side, the valley
"deer and moose"
"among the laurel, and the hemlock"
"and the pine,"
the river
abounding once with fish
a slow moving stream
of sewage, & refuse, & waste
now offends
                    or is a joke:
                    the "Lacky"
                    we laughed at as kids,
                    full of old tires, shoes, floating
                    condoms, rusted out junked
                    cars we used to sit in to
                    drive, on the banks
                    where we trapped rats
                    at the foot of Court St.
                    near Ella Burns's bar
                    under the bridge at
                    Albright Ave., so full
                    of stink & shit that a baseball
                    homered into the water
                    was unusable thereafter,
                    it was so fouled, we called it
                    an automatic out
five miles the city
its banks

PLAYING IN THE MINES

Jay Parini

Never go down there, fathers told you,
over and over. The hexing cross
nailed onto the door read DANGER, DANGER.
But playing in the mines once every summer,
you ignored the warnings. The door
swung easier than you wished; the sunlight
followed you down the shaft a decent way.
No one behind you, not looking back,
you followed the sooty smell of coal dust,
close damp walls with a thousand facets,
the vaulted ceiling with a crust of bats,
till the tunnel narrowed, and you came
to a point where the playing stopped.
You heard old voices pleading in the rocks;
they were all your fathers, longing to fix you
under their gaze and to go back with you.
But you said to them NEVER, NEVER,
as a chilly bile washed round your ankles.
You stood there wailing your own black fear.

GIVING IT UP FOR LENT

Edward Moran ⊞

Upon these coals I cast my curd
and on the crop from whence it rose
now fanned in the wind-whipped air,
I, stripp'd bare,
cleanse my lips but not my cup

parched with the last ashes of March
and all the froze cud-froth come forth
in fire and exceeding wroth

the message:
    blessèd
    are we and all now kirkless
    who in this ashheap of the living wordless
    keep silent station at the clotted cross
    at this, the rotted roodtime of the year
        sing *dairy air*

blessed, too, the colliers,
and the cheesemakers,
those that sift and those that sort

for none in grange and none in tipple
can unscaffold the dead rind from its breaker-beam shelf
then peel—no, roll away—the rock of the brimming word
so let the crop and the coal and the cream be fertile
        sing *allelulerry air*

THE DANCERS

Karen Blomain

Old Forge porches still have gliders that sigh
with the boring back and forth of summer nights.
In narrow backyards basil borders peppers, and
dusty tomatoes staked with pigtail rags wait to
ripen in the sun.

It's the town of Italian restaurants, famous high school
dance contests. The first time you won, wild copper hair

tumbled about your face as you left the floor.
Everyone clapped, your baby sister, she can really move.

Tonight we walk to town for pizza
past the gliding grandmas.
Muffled television from front doors open
in the summer heat trails us down the block.
We talk of the months we've been apart, your job,
children suddenly too old to be reason enough.
You confess you leave your husband sleeping after dinner,
drive two towns away to dance in a roadside bar.
When they ask your name, you tell the truth, Madonna.
They laugh and you do too—a different joke. But later
they are angry when you leave alone, elude the late night
pairings. No harm done, and you make sure to check the
rear view mirror, smart enough to take the long way home.

At family parties you and I always start dancing.
Soon the children join us and we twirl them senseless,
ourselves giddy with heat and wine. I've twirled myself
more times than I remember. Once I locked myself
in, danced and danced for hours, crying and shaking
until the lake threw its white morning face back into mine.
And I wasn't sure I could go on living any more.
Donna, how did the world get too small
for our wild dancing? I don't know
what to think about us when I see this careful
gliding and tomato rows, these quiet houses in Old Forge.
What we remember follows like a jealous partner
down this tired, ugly street. No wonder we forget
that youth was not the prize we'd won and got to keep.

DELAWARE LACKAWANNA DIESEL
RUNNING THROUGH

✺ Helen Ruggieri

In school Miss Black gets mad
when I don't know where the Aleutians are,
looking out the window watching
diesels pass, old women
in babushkas picking coal.

I live in the green house, in back,
and 18 steps up, between the road and
the tracks, level with the roadbed where
the diesel horn announces crossing
at the corner, two blasts, and the
windows shake,
every hour at night
tunneling darkness
past the barely floating island
I am, at sea, blue wallpaper,
and finally, I wake up
as if my whole life
depended on it.

The diesel horn
bellows toward the corner,
past slag heaps, culm dumps
to a cool blue place
without a name.

In the can't sleep diesel
every hour night
drifting past the calendar
I live by, following

a dream of an island
that knew what it had to be
and had to be found
or it didn't matter.

That diesel my clock—
wake up, wake up,
build an island.

AT THE COUNTING HOUSE OF
BUCK RUN MINE

for Frank and Vince

Harry Humes ◆

Past the high-boned faces
of the beautiful daughters of Minersville,
past the strip pits
with their fringe of laurel
and quaking aspen and white birch,
to this stone building,
windows smashed, floorboards pried loose.
We go up the narrow stairway
to the second floor,
afternoon light over closet and shelves.
One by one we squeeze through the hole
punched in the three-foot thick
stone and concrete wall of the vault.
Its steel door closed for good
in nineteen forty seven
when men in visors and arm garters
walked out for the last time,
their ledgers left in neat piles,
records of shifts, tunnels driven,

names of veins, Mammoth and Primrose,
the Buck, headings of breasts,
timber used in gangways, tons of coal.
Beneath our feet, mildew thrives
on paper fused a foot deep.
In such silence, we can find nothing,
no sign of uncle or brother or father,
nothing to explain night cough
or faces blue as blue bowls,
or what closed it all down,
women and children watching for years
the miners up and down the sidewalks,
their hands, their pale skin
so easily burned.

DOG HOLE

Thomas Kielty Blomain

I imagine him plotting
before he got old
how he would rob the mine
through a dog hole
beneath his house—
the condemned, now ruined
South Side home where
his family had lived for years

Before they shut off the power,
the heat, the water, the phone,
he must have spread out
stolen charts on the table alone,
searching for the closest vein

I imagine him then
starting to dig, filling wood pails
from the basement, dumping them
secretly outside, tediously,
like a prisoner tunnelling out

He had to have started long
before he got old, finally locating
the coal and chipping away;
dragging it out, two buckets
at a time, at a time when his triceps
would permit—crawling up backwards,
backing out through the hundred foot
black hole, spilling more each time now,
his arms boney and sore

Feeding the coal to his relic stove,
heating the house where he lived
at 77 alone in the dark, but for the
flickering anthracite glow

Officially condemned by concerned
Authorities, the place burned like
kindling one night, collapsing
on to the illegal shaft, claiming

the miner and his need to retreat
to the hole, another grief consuming
him as he scraped black heat beneath
the white winter night above

As they kicked away the smoldering frame,
they were all very surprised to find
such a dog hole in this day and age.

WALKING THE TRESTLE

🌲 Jay Parini

They are all behind you, grinning,
with their eyes like dollars, their shouts
of *dare you, dare you*
broken by the wind. You squint ahead
where the rusty trestle wavers into sky
like a pirate's plank. And sun shines
darkly on the Susquehanna, forty feet
below. You stretch your arms
to the sides of space and walk
like a groom down that bare aisle.
Out in the middle, you turn to wave
and see their faces breaking like bubbles,
the waves beneath you flashing coins,
and all around you, chittering cables,
birds, and the bright air clapping.

ROTTEN ANGEL

✦ Gerald Stern

My friends, still of this world, follow me to the
bottom of the river
tripping over roots and cutting themselves on
the dry grass.
They are all over on the left side, drinking beer and crying,
and I am there by myself waiting for the rotten angel.
For my sake it hasn't rained for twenty days
and all the old jetties are showing up again in the water.

I can reach my arms up into the second row of branches
and pull down clumps of dead leaves and barrel hoops.
I finally find my clearing and fall down in the dirt,
exhausted from thirty minutes of fighting for air.
I put an x on the ground and start marking off
a place for the gravel, the rhododendron and the iron bird.
My friends stand above me, a little bored by my death
and a little tired of the flies and the sad ritual.
—How I would love it if I could really be buried here,
a mile away from my house in this soft soil.
I think the state could do this for me—they could give me
a few feet of earth—they could make an exception.
I tell you it really matters and all that talk
about so many cents' worth of fat and so many grams
of water is really just fake humility.
I would hate being dusted on the ocean or put in a drawer
for perpetuity—I want to be connected
with life as long as possible, I want to disappear slowly,
as gruesome as that sounds, so there is time

for those who want to see me in my own light
and get an idea of how I made my connections
and what I looked at and dreamed about
and what the river smelled like from this island
and how the grackles sounded when they landed
in the polished trees and how the trucks sounded
charging up 611 carrying the culture
of Philadelphia into the mountains
and how the angel must have gasped as he swam
back to the shore and how he must have dipped
his head in the green water to escape the gnats
swarming after him in the dirty sunlight
a million miles for his New York and his Baltimore
and his Boston.

FOR A RUSSIAN MOTHER

Bim Angst

I

Baba was our closest tie, stringing us together
with Christmases and goobas—old men with spirits
in their beards, collecting for the poor.

She passed every Russian blessing
every Russian curse, through blood
and the mother tongue you both spoke
when you thought we did not understand
into the hands of the children,
all women.

II

You thumped my back.
Camel. Camel.
I dropped lower, afraid
to be seen deformed.
And you were just as afraid.
I was deformed from your side
perhaps unable to bear children
but then unable to carry further
the bent back, the narrow hips,
the cancer of watching a child grow wrong.

III

You are both vivid
when I bleed. I remember the first
rolled rags hidden in paper sacks.

I remember Baba showing me how
to wrap the torn white sheets
saying in Russian, this
is for us. Just for us. The men
should never know.

I remember you telling me too late
what to expect. And then, only stories
of what would happen: dogs would follow
then, there was a smell, I am still weak
at the sight of my own blood.

I can feel it start early, before
the flow, and I accept it the same way
you have come to accept
my weakness, packing me in
when I come home drunk, knowing
God is punishing you for some terrible sin.

TANYA

Jay Parini

One day after school
I was running the tracks
back into the country
in early spring, sunlight
glazing the chips of coal,
old bottles and beer cans
shoaling the sides. I ran
for miles, stripped
to the belly, dogwood
odors in the air like song.

When I stopped for breath
I saw there were women
bending in the ferns.
They spoke in Polish,
their scarlet dresses
scraping the ground
as they combed for mushrooms,
plucking from the grass
blond spongy heads
and filling their pouches.

But the youngest one
danced to herself in silence.
She was blond as sunlight
blowing in the pines.
I whispered to her . . . Tanya.
She came when the others
moved away, and she gave me
mushrooms, touching my cheek.
I kissed her forehead:
it was damp and burning.

I found myself sprinting
the whole way home
with her bag of mushrooms.
The blue sky rang
like an anvil stung
with birds, as I ran
for a thousand miles to Poland
and further east, to see her
dancing, her red skirt
wheeled in the Slavic sun.

MAKING SOAP

✺ Nancy Deisroth

I used to make my own soap,
made it of drippins, like lard, old
lard drippins; you'd save that and when
you had about four pound of drippin,
I'd get a can of lye, and dissolve
so much water, you know, cold water;
dissolve the lye in *cold* water,
'cause that thing boils.
You'd stir till it dissolved good.
Then that would be hot, so you'd leave it go.
If you put something in there it'd boil.

Then you'd get your drippins soft on the stove.
You'd put the can till it melted; the drippins
had to be melted, and when the lye
water was cold, you'd be stirrin and stirrin
these drippins, you know, into the lye
with a stick. You just kept goin and goin,
kept stirrin till that would start to settle.
When you saw it start gettin thick already,
then you couldn't stir it no more; you'd quit.

You'd want it smooth, so you'd leave it sit,
till about next day; it would be a bit soft.
You'd pour it into a big square pan.
You'd cut it, whatever size you want,
maybe a dozen, fourteen pieces,
then you left it another day or two,
and it got so hard, real good and hard.
I put paper between, newspaper, and piled

the soap bars one the top of another
in a cardboard box in the summer kitchen,
the shanty, you know, to keep it cool.

You'd use that, then, to scrub your floors,
and rugs, and workclothes, things like that.
It was really good soap for washing clothes,
like when rubbin them on the washboard, 'cause
it got the stains out, it really did, but
your hands would get red and raw from the lye.
It was strong; the lye in there made it strong.

So, you'd make soap. Some people did.
Some didn't even know how.

WALKING THE ANTHRACITE

Harry Humes ✺

It could be the rim of the world,
the rocks breathing summer,
the copperheads coiled brilliant
near the huckleberry bushes.
Below me, there could be a town,
row homes like teeth set too close together,
dust on all the windows.
And then there's the ravine with the small pool,
smells of ferns, birch, the wet undersides
of last year's leaves, the musk of last night's beasts.
There's an old coal mine, its tipple rotting,
tunnels caved-in for hundreds of feet
and wires strewn everywhere, cans of nails
rusting beside the old shack.

There used to be a man here, a father
with bad lungs and scar-blue knees.
I imagine him standing at his pit, the earth
thick on him, eyes gathering
all the light before he went down.
This ground could be my darkest blood,
its hot veins places I must crawl.
I think of my pregnant wife, her pregnant shape.
I am mined by fatherhood; I have broken my carbons,
dynamited my flesh, walked alone into these hills for days.
At night, by an old carbine lamp,
drinking the bitter hill water,
I feel the tunnels rising like charms to my flesh,
calming me, offering the lost pale face like long sleep.

GENETTI HOTEL

Craig Czury 🍁

Tonight you can breathe
and the mayflies aren't skidding cars
off the 8th Street bridge—there's a breeze.
Cooling Trend, Naida says last week in
Olyphant the day fat Eddie died—*such a good lookin'*
guy when he was younger; it was a shame
t'see 'im the way he let himself go like he did.
So stink'n hot I was up at 5, fixed myself
some elbows an' sausage, then scrubbed the walls.

But tonight you can breathe before sleep.
And if I sleep now early
I'll wake to catch the string-hair & mouth act I was
twenty years ago *hanggin out onda Square*
3 a.m.—*Them gawdam kids it's terrible.*

Every routine I invented those years I needed
so that now
when you see me studious at Donuts Delite
figure I'm writing any perversion of one of your
past-lives too: 16 and on the loose open shirt,
not a flyin' fuck across*t'jer skull . . . com'ere gimme a
smoke*
So fast this coffee granulates light,
my naked ladies at Bourbon Street can't hardly
dance without me now I'm looking at us.

ELVIS, MY LIFE, AND THE REAL MADONNA

❖ Maggie Chelland Martin

My entire life
every moment
welled up inside me and took form
    It stood next to me as I held the paper plate piled
  high
with fried dough drowned in granulated sugar
and listened to a scrawny young man trying to impersonate
  Elvis

He moved his hips (without the King's grace I might add)
on the portable stage
right there in the Chapel Yard for god sake!
facing the tent set up to shelter The Madonna they all
prayed to
so many years ago
resurrected now
in plaster of course

and presiding over the festival
after an absence of at least fifty years
There was much jubilation

My life and I watched it all as we ate the food we'd grown
     up on
the same food which in recent years had been labeled
nutritionally unsound
We chatted
after I got over my initial surprise at her presence
and stared at the faces we'd known forever
grown old
The people I had left behind were milling around us
beaming proudly
pinning dollar bills on the Madonna's tent flaps and paying
their respects before going on their way to sample their
favorite
lethal dishes
or buy chances for the drawing or try on genuine silver
jewelry
or watches made of gold

We watched
my life and I and listened to the laughter and the
greetings as we kept our distance
but soaked it all in
We were doing fine until "Elvis" began singing "Love Me
     Tender"
And then it was all over for my life
She began to rant about how awful the people had been to
     say what
they'd said about the "One and Only" who did they think
     they were
anyway? it didn't matter how he moved his hips just listen
     to him

56

sing! how could they be so unfair?
She went on
Something about his autographed picture that stared down
    at her
lovingly, she emphasized
from her bedroom wall in the old house
I don't need to tell you how shocked I was by her
unexpected outburst
I hesitatingly looked around in case anyone had heard her
It appeared no one had so I tried to calm her down
I asked if she'd like a cannoli or a cup of cappucino
maybe a seat in the shade
I told her I understood
After all my heart still melts when I hear that song
It held so much promise! she interrupted
Imagine the concept of somebody LOVING YOU
FOREVER AND THEY ALWAYS WILL
People built their whole lives on that promise!

There was nothing I could do or say
to stop her ravings
I licked my sugared fingers as I attempted to find a way
to deal with her
All of a sudden it came to me
I got rid of the plate and wiped the stickiness off my lips
and went to The Madonna's tent
Cautiously checking in case anyone saw me
I pinned a dollar bill on one of the flaps
Then I walked my life
firmly but lovingly
over to The Madonna
I figured she'd know what to do

III

"Bells like sad angels"

LACKAWANNA

W. S. Merwin

Where you begin
in me
I have never seen
but I believe it now
rising dark
but clear

later when I lived where
you went past
already you were black
moving under gasses by
red windows
obedient child
I shrank from you.

on girders of your bridges
I ran
told to be afraid
obedient
the arches never touched you the running
shadow never
looked
the iron
and black ice never
stopped ringing under foot

terror
a truth
lived alone in the stained buildings
in the streets a smoke
an eyelid a clock

61

a black winter all year
like a dust
melting and freezing in silence
you flowed from under
and through the night the dead drifted
down you
all the dead
what was found later no one
could recognize

told to be afraid
I wake black to the knees
so it has happened
I have set foot in you
both feet
Jordan
too long I was ashamed
at a distance

FATHER AND MOTHER

Anthony Petrosky ✿

"This is the place," he said, waving at the door.
"This is the place we used to meet."

My father,
his face slightly yellow and translucent
in the white light,
sipped his beer and sucked his teeth,
satisfied we had come here.
He was despondent,
because he couldn't change his life

and lived, he said, like a rat
trapped at the end
with a woman he didn't love
and with two kids
who wouldn't remember or care
that once he gave up the chance to be happy
or at least try
with a woman who loved him,
who made him talk.
Now wherever he goes, he remembers her—
turning a corner, tossing off her satin jacket,
walking arm in arm with him down Wyoming Avenue
in the dark on the sly. He has been in love
with her since the war.
Everyday he thinks of her.
"Who can understand," he says, "you?
And what good does it do me,
even if you do?"
Hammering at the table,
stuck in his old shoes
in his old brain,
he kept insisting,
"I'm not going to take it anymore,
one of these days—poof,
I'm just going to disappear."

*

It's funny, I have these images of him
peddling my bike like a Keystone cop,
working puzzles at the kitchen table,
and now with a handlebar mustache,
he looks remarkably like his father.
And we are alike:
we complain—

he about pain,
I about this:

Once, more than once,
late, very late, Friday after payday, he argued
with my mother, bickering over money, over
what she called "his stinking shitty house,"
what her life had become, the past,
her brother's insanity.
He accused her mother of killing her husband,
of nagging until his heart gave out.
They argued over the neighbors,
over who was whose friend,
over who talked behind his back.
"Who do you think you're kidding, Tony," she said,
"everyone knows you're a good-for-nothing drunkard,"
and he leered and lurched, and she pushed on,
until it filled the house, inflected
upstairs, dragging me out of bed,
pushing me between them, telling him to stop,
to leave her alone;
while my sister cried,
clinging to her
the four of us huddled,
until he walked away to drink,
and we went back to bed.
That night, I heard my mother inching down the stairs;
I followed her
and stopped to watch through the bannister—
he sprawled at the foot of the stairs, passed out.
At first, she called "Tony, Tony,
get up, go to bed, get up,"
then pulled at his arm,
and when he didn't answer,

went through his pockets,
taking the money, stuffing it
into her nightgown, all the while
whispering, "You bastard, you lousy bastard."

*

That yellow clapboard house
tilted toward the river,
and its papered walls
reeked of dogs
and a sourness
that made my mother sick.
She sat on the mohair sofa
chain smoking,
picking at her fingers,
while he rushed ahead,
remodeling.

During the night once,
after the walls had been gutted,
rattlings from the kitchen below
woke me. As I sat up to listen,
fear radiated from my stomach
to my arms and legs,
and when I
peered down the stairs,
the noises grew louder,
a dull thudding
in my head,
escalating,
until I jumped
or was pulled.
Trying to get up,

I heard his voice,
"Tony, Tony,"
coming closer,
"Wake up, wake up,
it was only a dream."

*

A dog barks.
A dog in a dream.
A neighbor's dog.
My father curses it.
It is him again,
leaning on Austin's fence
the day (I was nine or ten)
I ran for a priest to stop the fighting,
only he couldn't
anymore than I could,
although I had tried
by reading aloud from the bible.
They must have thought I was crazy
standing between them
in my underwear,
because they shut up a few minutes,
and I must have imagined the voice of God,
or myself bigger than the two of them.

*

Today he comes to me like a ghost,
malarial, shivering and sweating
in the old poster bed,
then it's winter again,
and he staggers home from Scoops—
my mother called it a "gin mill"—

66

with a lopsided Christmas tree
over his shoulder. She said
(I remember her exact words),
"your brain must be going bad
from all the boozing, Tony,
you can't even see straight anymore."
Furious, he chopped it into pieces,
then she went out, taking me along.
Picture the two of us,
carrying a tree in a blizzard,
my mother in rubber boots, her checkered coat,
an old brown wool scarf over her head,
me in misery.
He was asleep in front of the TV
when we got home,
and once we had the tree in its stand,
the argument began that went on
while my sister and I decorated;
and when, in a gesture, ma pulled us together,
that made him angrier.
He discouraged us from giving him gifts
and fussed irritably when we did,
although he liked fedoras
and handled them with expertise and grace
like a man who knew how to handle himself
in the company of men and women.

*

He says the past disappears and changes,
and as I look through old photographs,
trying to remember what it was like
out there in Exeter, across the street
from Joey John's Esso Station,
staring into the yard at him,

nothing comes back,
except the penetrating odors
of gasoline and oil;
yet I recall too,
from the same time, I think,
obese angels fluttering
between heaven and earth
in a catechism's blue sky;
and these photographs of him
and his brothers in uniforms
seem unreal, removed
from what I know about them.
In this once at the entrance
to the Air Force Academy,
Joe, arrogant, the youngest,
sits on a concrete bench
leaning forward,
his elbows on his knees,
a cigarette dangling from his hand;
and in another, Vince, the oldest,
short and stocky, poses
in combat fatigues on a tank's turret;

with a rifle by his side;
and in this scalloped-edged picture,
my father, relaxed,
his foot on a wooden locker,
a submachine gun
resting across his leg,
smiles beside a large Uncle Sam.
He went to Africa, France,
and then Germany with Patton,
but he has never said
what was going on with his life

when my mother's face was thin
and severe as it is here
where she stands in a long coat
in front of a Pullman car
with her arms around him, crying.

*

Twenty years later,
he worked on the line
while he built the house on the Susquehanna
where grandfather would row every morning
with his bamboo poles and wicker baskets
to fish without catching fish.
It was still dark when I went along,
the river poised in its sounds,
and we sat in silence
as he cast and cast.
He tried to teach me to swim too
without swimming
by standing behind me,
moving my hands in a crawl,
then he rowed to the middle,
and paddled away
as I dove in panic,
trying to catch the back of the boat
by swimming the only way I could,
underwater.
Almost twenty years later,
I attributed this to my father,
and remembering the distant
removed look
in grandfather's eyes,
gave that to him also.
And once in a foggy rain

in my father's slicker,
I rowed along the shore
in a boat slowly filling with water,
as two large luminous creatures, more like plants than
birds
shot with silvers and blues, faded in and out,
skittering awkwardly then gracefully over the surface.

*

The night grandfather died
we kissed him goodbye,
then listened to people telling stories
in the old language
in the kitchen.
My father, crying, stooped down,
wiping my face, and put him arms around me,
then told this story:

"Ma," he said, "had put up pickles in a large crock.
The basement, where the kitchen was,
smelled of vinegar.
She had just set the crock next to the stairs.
I was just a kid.
I was on my way to the kitchen
when Pa, coming back from the mines,
came in the side door.
I wasn't sure he saw me.
I stopped at the head of the stairs
when he stopped half-way down.
The next thing I knew, he was running
and cursing in Lithuanian.
I ran after him.
The cat had snuck in
and was taking a leak in the pickles.

Pa reached over and squeezed its neck.
When he looked up, he didn't say a word—
went right past me out the door
with the dead cat dangling from his hand.
Pa sure loved those pickles and hated that cat."

The return trip from the old train station in Pittston
stunk.
The humid air had the viscosity of grease.
Tiny white marble floor tiles had worn paths.
We had four suitcases and bags
filled with clothes, vegetables.
We waited on oak benches,
not talking.

*

Della, my mother's sister,
lived with them until my father threw her out.
Afterwards, my mother
sank into depths,
talking to the dead,
then to the radio my father bought her.
She never recovered
and talked more to the voices,
especially during bitter winters
when she invented a lover.
She saw him in church,
talked with God,
and turned to violence.
"I can't even make a fist
to fight back," my father said,
"See, arthritis has ruined my hands."
"I had rocks in my head when I married her,"
he grumbled as he looked up to see my reaction.

We were sweating from the heat and beer.
"Why do you argue so much," I asked.
"You don't know the whole story," he went on.
"She's crazy.
We're walking down the street,
and yakety yakety yakety,
she's talking to her radio,
so I told her,
'Why don't you go see a psychiatrist,'
and she grabs a stick from the trash
and starts hitting me.
Everyone's watching.
You don't know how mean she can get
when she starts frothing at the mouth.
One of these days I'll just call the cops
to take her away,
but what am I going to do at my age,
look for another woman?
I'd hang myself before I'd do that."

She couldn't sleep
or stop picking at her face.
He put her on valium and mood elevators.
A social worker showed up.
"I don't look for anything from anyone," she said, turning
    him away,
"and I expect the same."

*

We were visiting my parents.
It was August, hot.
Ma told Ben, who was three, to eat his beans,
"or you won't grow up strong like your father."
"No," he said, "I don't like beans."

"Here," She pushed at the beans with a fork.
"Ma, he doesn't want them."
"They're no good."
"Oh, no, they have lots of vitamins."
Ben put a piece of hamburger in his mouth,
chewed, looked up at my mother, and whined,
"I don't like you grandma Bernice."

Silence.
We stopped eating.
For a moment, I saw a procession around the table
with me in a top hat in the lead, waving a baton,
while Ben blew a trumpet as all of us
in medieval robes and gowns waved and sang in unison,
"We don't like you grandma Bernice, we don't like you."
When it faded, I was staring at my father.

"Ben tell grandma you're sorry."
"No."
She looked hurt.
"Ma," I said, "why do you keep niggling him?"
"Never mind," she answered,
"I don't want to talk about it."

*

One of those sultry days
before we had a car;
we rode with my uncle in his blue coupe
to the house on the river.
Ma sat in the front seat
staring ahead.
She must have distrusted us even then.
Early on, my father imagined
she couldn't handle money,

and since she didn't have a job,
she didn't have any.
They shopped at discount stores,
where he'd let her buy little things.

When she left, they were packed unopened
in cupboards and closets—
strainers, ladles, towels, trivets,
and piles of tupperware
stacked inside of each other
like pastel blocks.

AMONG SCHOOL CHILDREN

◈ Craig Czury

I've been waiting outside an office
  where a grown man is learning to speak correct
  enunciation
    and inflection of a language school children in that
    country
have the same way learned before entering school—each
    sound
chewed and lolled from his mouth like a sopping wet bird.
In another room the tapclack, then grinding print-out
of a computer word processor in a language never needed
to be spoken in love, or inflection—there are reasons
my grandmother refused to speak English in her sad new
    world.
I want to say: like a drawbridge I am waiting, stacking up
and jamming what's immediate in order to allow what
    flows natural
to pass under . . . But I've come here to complain
in my mother's irritable age of complaint, my

grandmother's
unintelligible voice from Pringle Hill, my father's spliced
    words,
And Murphy's Law chart I'm testing my vision with now
    the other eye
while waiting to speak out against a man, a poet from out
    of the Region,
who, in prefacing his original words: This next piece of
    shit
I'll read . . . in a community where to be a "poet" is such a
    brittle
risk among soon-to-be-out-of-work school children,
    prefaced
each one of our strenuous first attempts at
    flight—reminded me
how far away all of us drive our first birds of poetry
each time we open our mouths to speak.

LEARNING TO READ

Helen Ruggieri

She held up cards and said
the sound of the letters and
then we repeated the sound.

Then she held up cards
with small words:

COW   NOW   HOW

And we put the sounds together:

C like a small cough
in back of the throat

OW like the sound
of a hurt child
then we put them together:

COW   COW   COW

and there was a picture of
the huge beast staring.

N was nuh with the
tongue in back of
the teeth and the
same small child:

NOW   NOW   NOW

which was the difference between
tick and tock when the hands of
the clock moved, gone before you
could say it.

aitch is a puff in the mid
throat and that child
hurting again:

HOW   HOW   HOW

which was a way
or a question to ask
to find something out

COW   NOW   HOW

In that room with desks
nailed to the floor I
had a seat by the window

saying to myself:

> Cow is the beast

> Now is the time

> How is the way

looking out over the cindered yard,
the tracks, roofs, the very top of
the colliery chute, plumes of violet
from burning slag at the bottom of
the valley drifting far away—

> COW   NOW   HOW

a whole world through
those windows

FIRE

Maggie Chelland Martin

S pring winds were blowing hot
   early
   warning winds
    teasing
cracking open doors long shut
stirring up desires buried under winter snow
melting now
rising up
raising from the dead the longing to know passion
to be free

And I remembered the smell of burning
remembered watching fragments of paper
edges glowing orangey red
rising
riding waves of heat
floating down
into and around the metal trash can fragile
with rust
poked through with holes
on the bottom
the receptacle
keeper of the burnings

I'd stand rooted in early teen aged dusky summer evenings
watching the flames
waiting for the fire to die enough
to make it safe
then carry the heaviness
the heat inside me
to the pizza parlor
the new one on Main Street
where I'd sit with my up the street girlfriend
and listen to the mournful sounds of Gogi Grant's
"The Wayward Wind" come blowing through the jukebox
as we talked about the girls who . . . you know . . .
did it
but no . . . of course we'd never . . . no

PEDLAR

✦ Nancy Deisroth

A pedlar used to come to town,
his face and hands all flecked and scarred,
sketched and patterned in shades of blue.
A mine explosion had left him blind
so a boy would lead him from house to house.
He carried a wooden box, or tray,
with buttons, what-not, candies, thread.
Across his shoulders a leather strap
held the tray while he plied his wares.
His fingers were nimble and knew the tray,
proffered each small thing and took the coins.
Someone would put him up for the night; he'd pay
with a paper of pins, pieces of peppermint,
and tales of the mines before his eyes went dark.

BUYING PAGAN BABIES

Karen Blomain ✦

Five cents to move one step
up the Holy Childhood Association
hundred-rung ladder on the blackboard
of our classroom of St. Thomas School.
On a poster, their pictures—little moon
faces the color of clay, mushrooms, and tree bark,
children living in the wild.
Sister told us how the missionaries had to chase
those little children through forests

hung thick with snakes and vines you couldn't tell apart
to get them dressed in waists and trousers
and teach them to kneel. Even years later she got letters
from a friend she went to school with,
listening to God as they walked arm-in-arm
down the dusty road from chapel.
That was as much excitement
as Sister Dominick wanted in her life.
Though her friend begged and she told us she cried
when Sister Mary Ellen left, she could not make herself
cross the water. When the monthly letter came,
as a special treat, chair in place
and every blackboard perfectly erased, her habit settling
like black sails becalmed she'd read to us
from pages shaking in her chalk-white hand
about the other life she could have had
and the children that we somehow owned.

BOTTLED-UP

Maggie Chelland Martin

Maybe if I just let it out
all the stuff dammed up inside for God knows
how long
all the thoughts I've thought or the things I've
wanted to say
but I haven't had the courage to come right out and
actually say
so they stick somewhere inside me
making me think of the labels on the labeling machine
in my father's soda plant

A sticky gooey not so awful glue got spread mechanically
on the back of each label and placed and tamped down on
    the bottles
But sometimes the labels would stick to each other
and big chunks of what used to be separate labels
would gum up the works
and you'd have to clear them out and start all over again
Or when the bottles went upside down on the line
into the bottle washing machine
Two by two all in a row they'd move through the opening
covered with rubber curtains that separated
inviting the bottles to go inside to be sprayed and scrubbed
bubbled up bright and clean in a bath made of soap suds
    and lye
or something so caustic it burned if you got it on your
    hands
In went the bottles and out on the other side
Unless there was a snag and a bottle broke
backing things up
bringing everything to a halt
Then my father would have to turn off the machine
and reach into that opening where the caustic shower
    showered
his hand searching in the darkness behind the rubber
    curtains
for the broken bottle that gummed up the works
sometimes he'd get cut
and after he'd found it he'd press the on button and begin
    again

I'd stand
as a child
in my rainy day rubber boots

covered with water
on hot summer days
and load cases and cases of dirty bottles onto the line
There was a rhythm to be kept
and a particular way to lift the bottles
turning them upside down
fitting them into the holes that would take them away to
    be cleaned
removing the traces of orange or red still left inside
The remnants of someone's wedding reception or a picnic
or quick cold drink after hard work in the afternoon sun
The final traces of a celebration or a conversation
that may have ended in unfinished sentences
unexpressed words
One after another case after case the bottles went on their
    way
their secrets going with them

They were picked up by my father
who stood at attention at the end of the line
He'd lift them up and examine them in the light
then place them right side up to be filled again with the
    colored syrup
streaming down the clear hose from the upstairs mixing
    room
where porcelain vats sat filled with just the right
proportions
of magic ingredients mixed with the sugary solution
oil of wintergreen
cherry extract
gingery ginger
lemon and lime
Each bottle was filled with the sweet water on its way to
    the spigot

that pumped in the carbonated water
and then it was proffered up to be capped

The caps were kept in bins alongside a wall near the
    bottling machine
Individual compartments filled with caps for each flavor
They looked like sparkling jewels
and made a special clacking sound when I stuck my hands
    into the pile of them
Hundreds of corklined fluted metal gems
scraping against each other as I scooped them up
and let them rain down on themselves
I can still feel the coldness of the metal
the dull sharpness of the fluted edges
the softness inside of the clean brown cork

After the bottles were capped
my father would take them off the machine
and deftly place them in awaiting cases made of wood
painted on both sides with the words "Chelland's
    Beverages"
They'd be moved to the other side of the plant
labeled and stacked
then loaded onto the delivery truck
it was red and had two tiers open on all sides
Sometimes in winter the bottles would burst in extreme
    cold
decorating the truck with cascades of multicolored ice

My father had hoped for sons
to pass everything on to
His work
His name
He had none
So he sold the business

He went on for a while
managing other people's soda plants
　　But
When did it start for him?
　　You know
The gumming up process
the holding it in so it gummed up the works
'till he died

NANTICOKE BUS

Craig Czury

J ust as the wind pulverizes
　　a layer of snow off the overhang
　　you step down into slush.
What else
within these eighteen minutes
along the Askam road
to moan about besides the bitter cold?
Besides the roadcrews
and the terrible "auteritis"
where they took out *here look*
the stitches.
Dem two on walfer
wit'da big dog t'feed shackin' up

This room I rent on the corner
above the bus stop
could have once been on wheels
and junked for scrap with its
body smells and stains wherever you sit.

According to schedule
each day all of you come to gather
      with your Le Bags
      outside my window
      which could have been a door
      for you to step up
      and grunt into the way I hear you
      safe among yourselves
      talking about how shabby he lives.
      Thirty-six and never been married?
      Well, ya see 'im out walking'
      God-knows all hours,
      must be runnin' from som'tin.
      And why's he need t'be alone so much
      anyway?

      Ya know, he don't work an' yet
      yaz always see' im sittin' around
      drinkin' coffee.
      It's a damn good t'ing
      about his father dead ya know . . .

HOSPITAL VIEW

Karen Blomain 🍁

Tonight darkness sifts down from the mountains,
wide hips around the anthracite valley.
Below this window decayed row houses bulge
with poor switching off the day. A Viet Nam vet
lives at the corner, collects his pension and spends
the month driving a yellow VW through his private jungle.
Even from this distance winter's

hard-bodied, the sludge and ice at street corners stiffen,
ice aglitter like coal under streetlight.
As teenagers we couldn't wait to leave a town
that had worn our parents lives away. In backyards filled
with children and tomatoes, sopped wash struggled
in the wind and we planned better lives
while television hooted through dark
waves of steaming cabbage and complaints.
We use the word *stuck* for what would happen
if we didn't leave and thought of wide open
butterflies impaled on pins in the Everhart Museum.
So we went as far as luck would take us,
into one jungle and not quite back
or like me, wrecked and wakeful
in the scant comfort of winter's sorry light.

THE RED COAL

Gerald Stern 🏵

Sometimes I sit in my blue chair trying to remember
what it was like in the spring of 1950
before the burning coal entered my life.

I study my red hand under the faucet, the left one
below the grease line consisting of four feminine angels
and one crooked broken masculine one

and the right one lying on top of the white porcelain
with skin wrinkled up like a chicken's
beside the razor and the silver tap.

I didn't live in Paris for nothing and walk
with Jack Gilbert down the wide sidewalks

thinking of Hart Crane and Apollinaire

and I didn't save the picture of the two of us
moving through a crowd of stiff Frenchmen
and put it beside the one of Pound and Williams

unless I wanted to see what coals had done
to their lives too. I say it with vast affection,
wanting desperately to know what the two of them

talked about when they lived in Pennsylvania
and what they talked about at St. Elizabeth's
fifty years later, looking into the sun,

40,000 wrinkles between them,
the suffering finally taking over their lives.
I think of Gilbert all the time now, what

we said on our long walks in Pittsburgh, how
lucky we were to live in New York, how strange
his great fame was and my obscurity,

how we now carry the future with us, knowing
every small vein and every elaboration.
The coal has taken over, the red coal

is burning between us and we are at its mercy—
as if a power is finally dominating
the two of us; as if we're huddled up

watching the black smoke and the ashes;
as if knowledge is what we needed and now
we have that knowledge. Now we have that knowledge.

The tears are different—though I hate to speak
for him—the tears are what we bring back to the
darkness, what we are left with after our

own escape, what, all along, the red coal had
in store for us as we moved softly,
either whistling or singing, either listening or reasoning,

on the gray sidewalks and the green ocean;
in the cars and the kitchens and the bookstores;
in the crowded restaurants, in the empty woods and
libraries.

MORNING, YEARS AFTER THE MINING

Thomas Kielty Blomain 🕷

At your leisure, you can grow
to love the early morning,
when the stillness is thick
and the blare of a horn rips
the calm like a bomb blast

Driving to town just after dawn,
especially in winter, is to feel
something of the hard past
(that I only pretend to claim),
when miners woke and shook
their cold bones from stuffed
mattresses on coarse wood frame beds,
sheathing themselves in yesterday's
clothes again to head out to another
long day where only ghosts escaped
from the silhouetted smokestacks
probing the thick morning air.

These smokestacks, and the spires
on the churches where wives prayed,

to this day finger the gray sky.
(Arthritis and history rhyme
in some way.)

The outline of this town against
the dull morning is testament
to them, those who descended
the dark shafts to strip the core
like termites in a tree,
their bravery unsurpassed, without
the intention to excel or succeed,
but only to feed their families,
and not even well at that.

To their grand memory is the bland,
jagged skyline of Scranton,
appropriately. And these mornings.
No shiny monuments could do.

BELLS LIKE SAD ANGELS

Craig Czury ❖

I just remember the voice biotone
and singing nothing I could really see,
only a lot of colorful glass stained
pictures of hippies.

And Orthodox Russian Christmas bells:
The Volga Boat Song—

where bells like sad angels
drone off our block houses into slag.

They named this old coaltown Welsh

for the doctor who rescued *Rooski* miners
early with his tonic: sugar whiskey
with dye

It's Sunday.

And I'm up over Summit Street
rummaging through the dump for Jimmy Hoffa
driving my old Dodge around the lid
of a Campbell's soup can.

Everything here you need for your backyard:
this huge wooden cable spool, batteries,
tirefuls of junk aluminum . . .

A good day after rain to climb around
the Lorree Breaker, or just walk the tracks
down where the D&H blew open a coalseam
and laid bare the face of a woman—

coal chin, forehead and nose of a woman
weeping real mud-ice tears.

THE MINER'S WIFE LEAVES HOME

Karen Blomain

The only way out
is by train,
the whistle
that muscles its way
into your sleep.

Leave the bed
quietly, go barefoot

through the grass,
then run along-
side, (your heart
will want to pop
its cage)

and desperate, begin
this song: You can take
          nothing,
          not the earrings paired
          for the night in their safe
          compartments, not the moon
          shaped nail clippings,
          your brush matted
          with hair,
          or the heavy locket
          of photos.

          Don't look back
          for smoke rising
          or wonder if you left
          the tap running. Let your legs
          gain air, until they
          are wings. Grab the rail
          and hold tight. Close
          your eyes against cinders.

          When the heavy boots,
          the flashlight
          discover you, reveal
          no history,
          bleach yourself white
          and stare,
          don't ask questions,
          don't imagine destinations.

A CHRISTMAS POEM

Helen Ruggieri

Our parents spoke languages from
countries that disappeared in the war.
We were the translators, their hopes,
overfed, indulged, rough
and Christmas made us pulse
like small tree lights.

The building was old and
we were young, too many
of us sharing books and desks;
our poor teachers added ruffles
to their skirts to imitate
Dior's "new look."

We exchanged our dollar gifts,
ate cookies from a dozen countries
with our nickel milk and then
they'd move us up to 309
and pull the blackout shades:
that old projector whirred and flapped

and in that mote-filled arc of light
came fuzzy Scrooge and we'd settle down,
forget the smell of damp wool,
whistling radiators, who didn't give us what,
and watch how we should share, make merry,
and every year we'd march
upstairs to 309 and watch again,
lest we forget.

THE PHOTOGRAPH

Harry Humes 🌲

1.

Maybe it is Easter, 1940
He has my brother in one arm
and me in the other
There are some swings and a pigeon coop
in the background
He has been coughing for days
into his red-flecked handkerchief
and his breathing
sounds like sleet against a window

2.

I think of him folding his napkin neatly
into his lunchpail then rising on thin legs
and walking down a gangway
through the dusty air

3.

Do I hear him now at the front door
then the back Does he climb the side steps
and knock softly on a window
I don't know
in the photograph
he seems like a man thinking of nothing
but holding his two small sons

IN ANDY GAVIN'S ON ST. PATRICK'S DAY

Thomas Kielty Blomain ❋

I sat in Andy Gavin's on St. Patrick's Day
After the parade drinking stout,
Watching the prison do nothing,
    Holding a paper against Long Kesh
Someone had handed me out of the crowd.

I read it in the sunlight through
The window which frames the jail,
And laughed with my friends at the tipsy language,
So Irish and quaint, forgetting
With my comfortable beer.
JUSTICE PEACE FREEDOM DEAR FRIENDS,
Was the salute, and what followed told
What they do. Those British
Slap their captives' genitals. It's hard
to believe but true, it says

They threaten to shoot them
In a lonely place, it says
They'll hand the lands over to the UVF
And punch them in the head
Or kick them if they like.

The British are a brutal lot,
That's sure. They use prods
On Catholic balls, it's hard
To believe but true, it says.
But not what for. An innocent

Irish lad wouldn't do anything he couldn't
Confess, so I think the British

Have built Long Kesh and it's St.
Patrick's Day, and there was just a parade
In honor of the old snake driver.

HACKING AND SMOKING

Craig Czury ❁

S he doesn't want to go yet,
the way she takes her time standing up,
those dark, sad eyes, the way she's draped
her coat, then tugging it over her arm
stares at the window. She's got a lot on her mind.
And we've made her more nervous by watching
how alone she is. Wasn't I suppose to
lose my mind to her when she walked in
out of fog this dark, those eyes?
It doesn't stay dark as late since Sunday
but I still wake with the hacking,
hike on my boots and walk across the Square
to sit among the old dead-peckers who have
woken themselves hacking up their black lungs,
drink coffee until the buses start,
hack and smoke our lungs into anthracite.
But it stays cold later. And maybe she's not
staring at the window so far away
but behind her at all of us, how alone we look.
Not even 5:30 a.m. when we glance nervous
away from ourselves in the window
and she hesitates at the door. In the glass
I know she's looking at me, then walks out.
Wasn't I suppose to wonder if maybe this one . . .

EASTER

Bim Angst

Dark. Words are not enough. I kiss
the icon twice. Once because I have always
and once for the children. The saints
in the ceiling see it is good. The candles
for the dead go a little brighter.
I do not want to move.
The priest pulls my arms. I must close
the space in line and march. We are all quiet now.
Outside I light my candle from a child's and pick
my place in the line for blessing. All the spaces
in the basket are filled with pisanki—the eggs
Christ bled on from the cross—and all we have gone
without these weeks: kielbasa, ham, milk
and the blessings for this day, the paska, hrutka, hrin.
When I move the handstitched doily I am filled with all
the smells.

The priest swings burning incense on a chain.
He covers the baskets with fine ash and with each
asks for the youngest children. We say they are well,
home waiting to be woken for this food.

We stand quiet waiting for the sun to rise
singing only when the priest comes round the church to
    lead
the banner train of saints carried on the shoulders
of our boys. Their robes are red and white, their hair
is combed with blessing oil, their shoes are shined.

We all wait for the dawn standing in the yard
before the grave, watch for the signs the sun will rise
look for those signs that every morning tell us we are
    saved.

GOING FOR WATER

Nancy Deisroth

One of my chores was goin for water,
and bein a girl didn't get me off light.
Strong as the boys, I could carry two buckets
at once, and brim full, without spillin a drop.
And I was an expert at primin the pump
with a cupful of water. (It don't take much,
except when the winter has stopped it with ice.)
Then I'd work that handle hard and fast
and watch the water jump from the spout.

The pump was three houses down from ours,
out in the street, for us all to use.
Folks up on Back St. had pumps in their kitchens:
Irish, mostly, the bosses, you know,
and Machellas, of course, with the boardin house
and all their kids (was it eight or ten?).
But we had to carry all of our water,
and keep it in boilers out back on a bench.
One of them things held six or eight buckets,
so three or four trips to the pump, I was done.

I fell only once, on some ice in December,
carryin water to prime the pump,
boilin water, for the pump was frozen;
and when I fell, I scalded myself.

I remember I screamed, and ran home cryin,
slippin on ice and the dirty snow,
my face and hands burnin and cold all at once.
Ma's face went white and I thought she'd yell,
but she didn't, just stripped off my wet clothes.
She wrapped me in towels, put salve on my burns,
then she sang to me softly and rocked me to sleep.

CONFESSION

Bim Angst ✿

I

My tongue rolls inside my mouth on Saturday.
All morning while I bake bread I cannot speak.
I form in my mind the words in English
for the sins I have only known here.

I take a long time pinning my hat
make the words to the mirror
the lips moving the right way. No one
will see them move when I speak these words.

On the way I pull the veil over my face
the air moves out of my mouth
the words become themselves, what I mean them
to be, on the other side of the net.

When I reached the churchyard I am ready.
Father Slepecky's dog moves along the fence with me.
The dog does not bark
born that way on purpose.

Inside I kiss the icon and kneel.

II

Dear Father, forgive me
for not baking bread for funeral
for breaking my fast last Friday
for slapping my smallest child.

Forgive me no flowers on my husband's grave
for telling old Mrs. Kotchko she is fat
for shooing neighbor children from my yard
for saving milk from the big ones.

Forgive me, Lord, for blame and wishing
forgive me waiting to go to school
forgive me sending my daughters to factories
forgive me not wanting to send another son to war.

Forgive me for coffee and wine
forgive me for oranges
forgive me for two pair of shoes.

III

A velvet drape on the confessional dark dark blue.
Inside a small shelf to sit on stuck to the wall
no room to bend my back. The priest is moving
papers on his side, in the grate I see his cloth
I see his shoes someone has shined.
The priest speaks Russian in Father Slepecky's voice

but I never call him Father Slepecky, never ask
for Hanya his wife. I never see his hands but I know
he pats his knees when I say good things.

He asks have I done penance, have I cared well for my
    children

99

have I honored my dead. He asks have I sinned sins I
    know
Will I be forgiven for sins I do not know. The priest asks
if there is peace now in my world, and to all this I answer
    yes.

He forgives me my list of sins and I leave holding a new
    mass card
the boy outside gives me to honor the new dead this week
Chiranko's boy run over by the train and an old woman
dead in her yard pulling the last tomato plants.

IV

"From the face of the vein"

THE HARVEST

🦢 Karen Blomain

In August we can, the last chore
before school. Fruit and vegetables
chosen curbside at dawn from the huckster's
truck or picked fresh from the kitchen patch
to chop, peel, stir, skim the dross, cook
down. Nanna lays on the orange rubber collar
taps once to seal. The jars clatter and clang
like dancers in a wild boil atop the stove.
Behind the thick door, a dirt floor, the cold
air a muzzle, silent in the spidery light
of a hung bulb we work. Amid ancient webs,
rows of mason jars gleam a rainbow: peaches
and pears, sweet cherries like clotted eyes
bobbing in their liquor. Above, all manner
of green—leaf and bean, chunked, cubed,
sliced and pickled. Chow-chow confettied
red and piccalilli—summer light
for a February table. We do it right:
clear the webs, line the shelves with brown
paper, then wash last year's jars.
The walls weep for our efforts.
Sometimes fragments of voices, miners
working inside the shaft just feet
away, float toward us on the moist air,
the scrape of tool and long grunt
at the heft. Burrowed in the glisten
of anthracite, they struggle with elements
older than language. Nanna starts
the tone she comforts with: Tura-lura-lura,
tura-lura-lie, and behind the wall a true

tenor holds the last note sure as any canary.
At the whistle, down from the breaker
they come, blinking at clouds
veined with peach-tinted light. Arms and torsos
stiff with dried silt, they nod to us on the porch
cleaning tomorrow's batch. We count the cars,
each a small hill of coal, as the 4:15
drags out of town, our hands snapping,
our aprons filled with the last summer green.

HUCKLEBERRY WOMAN

W. S. Merwin

Foreign voice woman
of unnamed origins nothing
to do with what I was taught
at night when it was nobody's
you climbed the mountain in back of the house
the thorn bushes slept
in their words
before day you put on
the bent back lie a hill
the hands at the berries

and I wake only to the crying
when the wash tub has
fallen from your head and the alley
under the window is deep
in the spilled blue of far ranges
the rolling of small
starless skies and you turning
among them key

unlocking the presence
of the unlighted river
under the mountains

and I am borne with you on its
black stream
oh loss loss the grieving
feels its way upward
through daggers of stone
to stone
we let it go it
stays we share it
echoed by a wooden
coughing of oars in the dark
whether or not they are ours
we go with the sound

THE BOOTLEG COAL HOLE

Harry Humes ◈

In mid-morning light over laurel and birch,
I'd carry my father's bologna sandwich,
thermos of tea, a bag of Welch cookies,
    up the path to the pit. There was an old Ford
bolted to a log foundation, a cable winding
from a spool on the back axle up over a tipple,
then down into the hole with its narrow rails.
It was how my father and uncles were hauled up,
the driver watching chalk marks along the cable
every hundred feet of the mine car's rise.
I'd sail pieces of slate over the spill bank
into the slush dam, or sit in the Ford

with the man too old to work inside,
who'd cough and spit into a blue handkerchief.
Or I'd climb the tipple up to where someone
had put a flag, and look into the pit
or down the tin chute to the dump truck.
Far below in the town, my house with its gable
and red shingles, high school and baseball field,
the creek always black beneath the four bridges.
When the buzzer sounded twice, the men
would come up, rattle and click of wheels,
voices rising thin as battery wire.
They'd sit in the shade with their sandwiches,
the bread smudged with dirt from hands and faces,
while my father, good with dynamite,
would crank a handle, and the ground would shake
with the afternoon's work blown loose
from the face of the vein.

MANGO

Karen Blomain

There was nothing exotic to name
in that coal town, still
we found words we liked the taste of
and used them as we chose.

When we said *mango*
we meant pepper—the green
or red bell pepper grown
in our kitchen patches. Shiny,
thick-skinned, hearty things
of flesh curving over airy chambers,

seeds hanging
in clustered arcs, neat
divisions in the dark interior.
I'm not sure how we came to call
them so, but remember still the shame
that day in Spanish class when
our teacher discovered, then ridiculed
our mistaken name for something common
as the dirt and potatoes
we were known for. The mango,
she told us, is an elegant fruit
grown only in special red soil.

ROBBING THE PILLARS

Harry Humes

"Pillars were columns of coal left
standing as supports for the mine tunnel."

Nervousness of eye and ear,
air like slate in my mouth,
pick and shovel heavy near fingers.
A half mile above, the mountain is green.
There are children, a woman,
the house with bright rooms.

Often in veins of coal
I have imagined sighs of the dying
cut off and at the last
eating wood and leather belts,
sulphur water turning their eyes ashen
with dreams of angels.

Carbide coats the chambered air,
buggies rattle narrow gangway.
My father was here years ago.
One by one, I rob the pillars he left,
haul coal away, watch the ceiling,
remember cool tiles of kitchens.

The tunnel creaks with bones,
brittle syllables, bad lungs.
Each hour passes like swamps turning carbon.
In the town, children clap hands.
The woman hears tons of balance
slipping from green plant to dark fossil,

and hears me as I begin, slowly,
to rise along a cable of light.
I have broken atoms of gravity
and will feel at my wrist all night long
hollows of blood, the great void breathing,
the tap, tap, tap of a last message on stone.

BONES & ASHES

Helen Ruggieri

Old women in babushkas walk along
the tracks with scuttles picking coal:
they winnow ashes, scatter them over
the icy winter walk.

They save bones from Sunday's meat,
boil them till the marrow makes broth,
give what's left to the dogs
to bury under the lilacs.

Dish water scrubs the floor, egg shells
and coffee grounds feed the earth for
potatoes, onions, cabbage, beets.
They waste nothing.

Their left hands fold over rosaries
count each bead twice as they work.
What sins do they covet—
profligacy, waste?

 ## PHOTO FINISH

Edward Moran

All that's left of my grandfather is this Ansco
            negative:
        a glassine stare, snapped at full lung,
            himself with cap and pick and carbide lamp,
                of the royal line of Galway
                bred of the wind's keen alchemy.

Breaker-boy bred and broke
        (twenty-five cents a day and an orange at Christmas
        from some Presbyterian do-goodstress
        who warmed her cockles and her Irish maids
        for six dollars a ton).

Pitched, in full array, down a gas-clotted shaft
        before the inspector came through.

I will not develop you, though.
        You have had enough of chemistry and agitation,
        you whose stars are black diamonds

set in a seamless white void,
your darkey face smudged with faith's bright
minstrelsy.

Now you belong to the ages,
carboniferous,
pressed,
a negative in earth's album.

Mine, o mine.

COAL PICKERS

Harry Humes ◈

They walk the steep mine road at first light,
stopping for breath by laurel or spill bank.
They touch slate or stir dark pools
of water with walking sticks.
All day their fingers curl around coal.
Do they feel the old swamp?
that killing ice? the smoldering silence?

I sit now in my own ashen dusk
and hear feet scraping shale or old timber.
What they whisper near the old tunnel
is what I have remembered for years.
I turn with them as they turn toward home.
Buckets filled, the sky around them like cold grates.

BARON LEGACY ✵

Thomas Kielty Blomain

They cut away a whole side of the West
Mountain overnight with big yellow
machines,
laying out huge rolls of gray plastic
like old bedsheets over vast heaps
of fresh trash dumped like war dead
by blue trucks at dawn and spread
by loud dozers and backhoes over the brown
area covered just yesterday by a forest
of old green trees.

Thick with new flies, the tight air
of the condensed sky over the slope
on the southern side seems a quivering beige
in the harsh summer sun.

Of course, no smoke rises from the piles
as it did from the culm of years gone by;
the flickering red and white and blue
of smouldering, pungent, huge, unused mine
product along the highways is mostly gone.
But if you allow your mind to wander past
the date to another page in the thick,
dirty book of our history, you can picture
new barons, who instead of taking out
of the earth are putting something back.

Tactful as politicians, in the paths
of their forebearers, they are modest
when we give them thanks.

SICKNESS

Bim Angst

I

The doctor lays his hands in all the places
my body readied for children, up into the rooms
I cannot see but know are there. He sees there
a sickness my body cannot fix itself.

Now the women of my family are around me.
A nurse sees what they have done is good. The hair
of my body in little pads placed in a sack
all the food my body cannot take washed into a pan.
The nurse says my women will take my wedding ring
but no one of us can get it off my finger.

My head is wrapped. I am naked in a sheet
counting backwards from a hundred and I catch myself not
    to say
in Russian what I have practiced long to say in English.
The doctor lays his hand on my head. He counts too.

II

I am awake. Father Slepecky's voice has woken me
the sound of his cross metal on metal on the rim of my bed
his hand too on my head. He is praying prayer
I would not know how to pray in English.
He says my god is with me.

I know now I cannot sit up
I cannot breathe without pain. I can smell nothing

but iodine and bandage. Nothing but white thin cloth
tied round and round me where once were the tops
of my inside rooms. I know, they have told me, what is
gone.

THE WHEELS OF THE TRAINS

W. S. Merwin

They are there just the same
            unnoticed for years
            on dark tracks at the foot of their moutain

behind them holes in the hill
endless death of the sky
foreheads long unlit
illegibly inscribed

the cars
have been called into the air
an air that has gone
but these wait unmoved in their rust
row of suns
for another life

ahead of them
the tracks lead out through tall milkweed
untouched

for all my travel

CARBONDALE CAVE-IN

Karen Blomain

That night the earth shrugged, cracked
like a hollow egg, the mine's
wooden legs gave way and part
of Salem Road disappeared.
The wavering and luminous cave-in
of our dreams. Pit and shaft,
we had imagined, rehearsed the sound,
rent of wall, heave and rain
of silt. But more softly
than we'd expected the ground
bolted, sagged, and swallowed two
front porches, a common patch
of walk, a yard, and half a living
room. In a lantern's deep blush,
the town stood behind sawhorses
to watch the family
misfortune had chosen. Empty handed,
single file they came, their faces
sheepish at the quick celebrity,
thinking maybe it's a curse
for past mistakes or fate to be housed
atop the honeycomb of empty
chambers. They navigate a crooked
funhouse stair, cross a makeshift
gangplank and fall
into the eager crowd. "Whose fault
is this," the father asks, "shoulda left
more down there." A procession
of cars circles the block, each window
full of greedy refusing eyes.

Pink blossoms and grey
doves cling to wallpaper trees
against the stare of floodlights.
We take the children to spin
all night on neighbors' sofas
rehearsing what they'll tell in school.
Some men steal back, to gape
at the blank windows, the sideboard,
its teapot and a wedding
photo, the stiff chagrin of lace
curtains ruffling in the wind,
the deep scar where the earth
began to pay itself back,
then creep home to check
the thermostat, the sleeping rooms.

THE MINER'S WAKE

❧ Jay Parini

in Memoriam: E P.

The small ones squirmed in suits and dresses,
wrapped their rosaries round the chair legs,
tapped the walls with squeaky shoes.

But their widowed mother, at thirty-four,
had mastered every pose of mourning,
plodding the sadness like an ox through mud.

Her mind ran well ahead of her heart,
making calculations of the years without him
that stretched before her like a humid summer.

The walnut coffin honeyed in sunlight;

calla lillies bloomed over silk and satin.
Nuns cried heaven into their hands

while I, a nephew with my lesser grief,
sat by a window, watching pigeons
settle onto slag like summer snow.

ASTRONOMY LESSON IN ASHLEY, PENNSYLVANIA

Edward Moran

A ltar boys in coaltowns are taught
not
to let the Most Heavenly Host
drop
by dredging the gravity of tongues
and the levity of lungs
and wishing for Venus the morning star
to breast against the rail, not far
from where their golden patens float
at pillared cleave of coal-stripped throat.

But morning stars have all been mined
from breasts and hillocks just behind
this slab of altar raillery.
Pockmarked asteroids instead
with sagging orbits bid for bread
on this slab of sacred colliery.

So altarboys in coaltowns must
forge epiphanies in dust
as Supernova Host invites
guests to feast on anthracite

116

for they are taught
not
to let the Most Heavenly Host drop
by dredging the gravity of tongues
and the levity of lungs
and things all implacid
like pools of mine acid
and coal-rosary seeds
and sex like clutched beads
and placing a paten against the communicant's chin
like moving Hubble's mirror into place to catch the grin
of the soul, the glint of the coal,
as the priest launches a pure white disc into her black,
black hole.

THINKING ABOUT SHELLEY

Gerald Stern ✺

Arm over arm I swam out into the rain,
across from the cedars and the rickety conveyor.
I had the quarry all to myself again,
even the path down to the muddy bank.

Every poet in the world was dead but me.
Yeats was dead, Victor Hugo was dead,
Cavafy was dead—with every kick I shot
a jet of water into the air—you could see
me coming a mile away, my shoulders rolling
the way my father's did. I started moving
out into the open between the two islands,
thinking about Shelley and his milky body.

117

No one had been here before—I was the first
poet to swim in this water—I would be the
mystery, I would be the source
for all the others to come. The rivers of China
were full of poets, the lakes of Finland, the ponds
of southern France, but no one in Pennsylvania
had swum like this across an empty quarry.
I remember at the end I turned on my back
to give my neck a rest; I remember floating
into the weeds and letting my shoulders touch
the greasy stones; I remember lying
on the coarse sand reaching up for air.

This happened in June before the berries were out,
before the loosestrife covered the hills, before
the local sinners took off their clothes and waded
like huge birds in the cold water.
It was the first warm day and I was
laboring in this small sea.
I remember how I hoped my luck would last;
I remember the terror of the middle
and how I suddenly relaxed after passing the islands;
I remember it was because of Shelley
I dragged my body up, tired and alive,
to the small landing under the flowering highway,
full of silence now and clarity.

KULPMONT HEARSAY TALES
Craig Czury

I didn't really see this
but I heard it from somebody
who somebody . . .

A woman was killed one night
tied to a tree and set on fire
on the steep road leading to Minersville

Broad Mountain around 11:00
and every year on the same date
the same time as her death
you can see her on the hill.
If you're driving around midnight
your car will stall out.
If you go up to her
she will take you with her.

My dad told me that when he was young
he used to go swimming in a stripping pit
until a kid went swimming there at night
and drowned.
My dad said everytime he went back
he heard the kid screaming and splashing
in the water.

I heard there used to be a cabin
in the woods where an old man lived.
The old man suddenly disappeared
but they found him in the graveyard
3 years later digging up graves
and throwing the bodies onto a truck.
The police followed him
and they saw him hanging the dead bodies
up on crosses and burning them.

My great grandmother said
a man was hung upback on a tree
and on some days if it's foggy
you can see a man on a horse

with a rope around his neck.
And if you walk up to him . . .

       There's a cave in Marion Heights
       in the woods, the floor's cracked
       and snakes are down there.

       And if you take a shortcut through the bush
       a man jumps out: Do you like to dance?
       Let's see you dance! Of course he's drunk.
       But when you look down at the man's feet
       his shoes are cut off and his feet are hooves

My grandmother went to the cemetery
and was staring at my pop-pop's grave
when his body arose and walked toward her.
She closed her eyes and his body was gone.
3 days later she died.

My friend told me
his grandfather was hunting for rabbits
and was caught and hung by escaped convicts
and buried in the woods.
Now in the morning
you can see rabbits hung by their necks
on ropes.

       I heard there was a boy
       who went camping in the woods.
       He saw a squirrel sitting
       next to him.
       Then he went for some sticks
       to make a fire.
       When he came back the squirrel

was lying dead
in the same spot.

There's an abandoned mine near the breaker
where there's all kinds of animal bones
and carcasses and a box-like thing.
But nobody would go down to open it.

And that Indian in the cave up at Indian
    Rocks
when it caved in . . .
you can see him at night by a fire eating fish.

Mike Rusinko's dad's friend
was working in a mine when a big rock
fell on him and chopped off his legs.
Now on the same night you can hear
the cranes start up and you can hear him scream.

July about 3 blocks away from my house
in the pine trees
is a mattress
and at night you can hear an organ playing.
Some people think a man lives there
but when we go up at night
and hear the organ
we look all over the pines
and can't find nothing.
In the morning only a mattress.

(Special thanks to the Kulpmont Elementary School students.)

121

SO THE COAL WAS GONE

Thomas Kielty Bloman

So the coal was gone
and the country froze,
scarred from the scraping,
poisoned by the sulphur,
and children drown where they swim
in the summer that heats the rank river.

A dirty carpet over the hills unrolled;
the miner's helmet, old and rusted.

So culm mountains and slag
bear scrub growth now, all along
the highway that runs right through.
Passengers in cars sense malodor
through windows closed for the passing
asking where is this on the map?
Which black dot?

So black lung is a pension
coughing in the streets
where nurses walk and watch their feet
past the bars that still for a dime
offer the past
and various ways to forget.

So kids know anthracite by its name
and throw chunks of it at passersby,
laughing on the railroad tracks
and at the caboose going by
the city
slower than the rest of the world.

Contributors

BIM ANGST, journalist, poet, and fiction writer, grew up in the southern coal fields of Carbon and Schuylkill Counties, "in the traditions and light of a closely knit family life." She holds an M.F.A. from Bowling Green University and has been widely published. The recipient of an NEA Fellowship, she has also been a fellow at Yaddo. At present, she lives and writes in Hegins, PA.

"The Blind Man," "For A Russian Mother," and "Easter" appeared in *Salthouse*. "Confession" was originally published in *The Beloit Poetry Journal* and "Sickness" appeared in *The Southern Humanities Review*.

KAREN BLOMAIN holds an M.A. from the University of Scranton and an M.F.A. from Columbia University. A poet, short story writer, and translator, she teaches in the Professional Writing Program at Kutztown University. Her awards include the F. Lammot Belin Arts Award, two Pennsylvania Council on the Arts Fellowships, and PEN Fiction Awards.

Poems in this anthology have appeared in *The Painted Bride Quarterly*, *The Greenfield Review*, *Passages North*, *Louisiana Literature*, *Staten Island Review*, *The South Coast Poetry Journal*, *The Carleton Miscellany*, *Footworks Magazine*, *The Mulberry Poets and Writers Poetry Minutes and Anthology 1990* and *The Pittsburgh Quarterly*.

THOMAS KIELTY BLOMAIN is a native of Scranton and a graduate of Keystone Junior College and Dickinson College. In the tradition of Wallace Stevens, he works in the insurance field and writes poems of the people and events around him. Works in this anthology have appeared in *The Dickinsonian*, *Metro*, *The Endless Mountains Review*, and *The Mulberry Poets and Writers Poetry Minutes and Anthology 1990*. A resident of Waverly, PA, he was Treasurer of Mulberry Poets and Writers.

123

CRAIG CZURY is from the Back Mountain area of Wilkes-Barre. He is the author of seven collections of poetry: *Janus Peeking, Against the Black Wind, God's Shiny Glass Eye, Except. . . ,* and *Hacking and Smoking.* The recipient of many awards and fellowships, Czury has begun to expand his notion of poetry away from the printed page into dimensional environments: *Tattoo Haiku,* a mural; *Civilization Meltdown,* a poem sculpture, and his ongoing series of earth and sky wall voices in elementary schools throughout Pennsylvania. He edited *Fine Line That Screams,* an anthology of poems by inmates from his northeastern Pennsylvania Prison Poetry Project. He is currently at work on a collection of children's original games.

Poems in this anthology have previously appeared in *God's Shiny Glass Eye* and *Hacking and Smoking.*

NANCY K. DEISROTH was raised in New Hampshire and attended Pinkerton Academy, where Robert Frost had taught as a young man. For nearly thirty years she has lived in Hazleton, PA, where she became interested in the history of the anthracite region and its people. The poems included in *COALSEAM* are from a work-in-progress, **Cut by Coal,** based on oral histories of local miners and their families. Her first collection, *Blackberries,* was published in 1991 by Nightshade Press, and her poems have been published widely in literary magazines. She is a production editor for The Haworth Press.

HARRY HUMES, a native of Girardville, PA, teaches at Kutztown University and is the recipient of several awards, including the Devins Award for his first book of poems, *Winter Weeds.* He is the recipient of three Pennsylvania Council on the Arts Literary Grants, and in 1991 he was an NEA Writing Fellow. He is the founder and editor of the poetry journal *Yarrow,* which is published out of the English Department of Kutztown University. His other books of poems are *Robbing the*

Pillars, *Throwing Away the Compass*, *Ridge Music*, *The Way Winter Works*, and *The Bottomland*.

Poems in this anthology have appeared in *Black Willow*, *The Pennsylvania Review*, *Kayak*, *Midwest Arts and Literature*, *Raccoon*, and *The Elkhorn Review*.

Born in Scranton, **PAUL KELLEY** teaches at Vancouver Community College and lives in Toronto, where he is studying for a Doctorate in Philosophy and Education. In recent years, he has published poems, prose fiction, and works for performance on stage and radio, as well as essays on literature, culture, and education. Most recently, *Such silent* and selections from his book, *Only undo*, have appeared in *Island* and *West Coast Line* and *B. C. Monthly*. His new work is entitled *Material*.

Poems in this anthology are part of his manuscript, *Anthracite* (1981).

MAGGIE CHELLAND MARTIN, a native of Old Forge, PA, is a poet, performer, and producer. She is a graduate of East Stroudsburg University and a longtime resident of Shawnee-on-the-Delaware. She is the producer of Maggie Martin and Friends Series: Poetry at the Deer Head Inn, Delaware Water Gap and Women's Work in Five Movements, a multi-disciplinary show which was the recipient of a Performance Grant. She has also been awarded a Pennsylvania Radio Theater Fellowship for creating new forms in audio using poetry and jazz.

Poems in this anthology have won awards from Mulberry Poets and Writers and have been included in WVIA-FM Poetry Minutes in 1990 - 1995.

W. S. MERWIN is one of the world's foremost poets and translators. Many of his early poems, including several from his Pulitzer Prize-winning collection, *The Carrier of Ladders*, and his collection of personal essays, *Unframed Originals*, have as their subject his growing up in Scranton. Poems in this anthology are drawn from *The Carrier of Ladders*. In addition to the Pulitzer Prize, Mr. Merwin has also received numerous awards and honors including a PEN Translation Prize. In acknowledgment of his distinction as a poet, he was named a Fellow of the Academy of American Poets.

At present, Mr. Merwin lives in Hawaii and is deeply committed to working for and writing about environmental issues.

EDWARD MORAN, a native of Wilkes-Barre, now lives in Brooklyn and Mauch Chunk (Jim Thorpe). He wrote or edited more than 43,278 definitions in the Random House Dictionary of the English Language (1987), including "sift," "culm," and "seamless." He recently wrote a biography of filmmaker Christine Choy, published in Asia in 1995. Several of his hymns, which combine traditional imagery with contemporary social issues, have been sung in churches in North America, Europe, and Australia; some of them appear in *Human Rites*, published in 1995 by Ward and Wild in London. He is editing critical biographies of 2,600 authors for H. W. Wilson's massive **Twentieth Century Authors** series, available in print and CD-ROM in 1996.

JAY PARINI grew up in West Scranton where his family still resides. His books of poetry include *Anthracite Country* and *Town Life*. His novel, *Patch Boys*, is a sustained glimpse of life in the anthracite area. A widely recognized poet, novelist, scholar and critic, Parini has written about Theodore Roethke and Amos Oz and has published numerous book reviews and essays.

Jay Parini lives in Middlebury, Vermont, where he teaches at Middlebury College and the Bread Loaf Writers Conference and edits the *New England Quarterly*.

ANTHONY PETROSKY spent his childhood and adolescence in Exeter, PA, where his family was connected with the mining industry. His first book, *Jurgis Petraskas*, received the Walt Whitman Award from the Academy of American Poets, a Notable Book Award from the American Library Association and a nomination for a Pulitzer Prize. His awards include a National Endowment for the Arts Writing Fellowship, a Pennsylvania Council on the Arts Fellowship, and a MacDowell Colony Fellowship. With his family, he has lived in China and Bulgaria and traveled extensively throughout eastern Europe. Currently he teaches at the University of Pittsburgh.

HELEN RUGGIERI grew up as Helen Mitchell in Mayfield and Peckville, PA. Her work has been widely published in journals and magazines and her books include *Concrete Madonna* and *The Poetess*. At present, she teaches at the University of Pittsburgh at Bradford and holds an M.F.A. from the Pennsylvania State University.

Poems in this anthology have appeared in *The Endless Mountains Review, Outerbridge*, and *Susquehannock, An Anthology*.

GERALD STERN was born in Pittsburgh and has spent much of his life in Pennsylvania. One of America's best-known poets, his books include: *The Piney's Rejoicing, Lucky Life, The Red Coal, Leaving Another Kingdom*, and *Selected Poems*.

A member of the faculty of the Writers' Workshop, the University of Iowa, he has received a Guggenheim Fellowship and two National Endowments for the Arts Creative Writing Grants and numerous other prizes. Poems in this anthology are from *The Red Coal*.